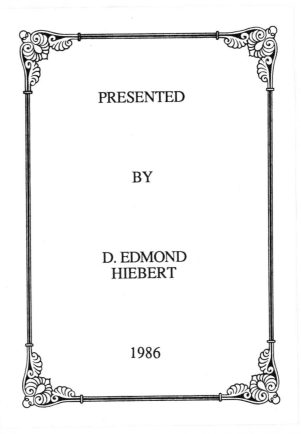

PRESENTED

BY

D. EDMOND
HIEBERT

1986

HELL IS NO JOKE

by

EVANGELIST ROBERT L. SUMNER

SWORD OF THE LORD PUBLISHERS

Murfreesboro, Tennessee

HELL IS NO JOKE
Copyright 1959 by
Zondervan Publishing House
Grand Rapids, Michigan

ISBN 0-87398-352-1

Printed in U.S.A.

Dedicated to the Mother of My Five Children
ORPHINA M. SUMNER
*Named for a French flower, the beautiful fragrance
of her sweet Christian life and testimony has been
a constant source of encouragement and inspira-
tion to me in my evangelistic ministry. God
was exceeding gracious in allowing me to
have her consecrated companionship, for
which I give Him humble thanks.*

APPRECIATION

Grateful acknowledgment is made by the author for the kind permission of *The Sword of the Lord*, a weekly magazine on whose pages most of these messages made their initial appearance in print, to reproduce them in this more permanent form. The writer of this book, formerly the Associate Editor and now a Contributing Editor, wholeheartedly and enthusiastically recommends that faithful periodical to all who read these sermons. Considering it the outstanding evangelistic journal of our time, I sincerely wish it were going into every home in the world.

Thankful appreciation is also hereby expressed for permission to quote the following copyrighted material: to The Rodeheaver Company for "Have You Counted the Cost?" by A. J. Hodge, and "Down by the River-side"; to the Nazarene Publishing House for "Have You Counted the Cost?" by Harland Fitch; to the Evangelical Publishers for "Heaven" by Annie Johnson Flint; to Grant Colfax Tullar for "Face to Face" by Mrs. Frank A. Breck; to The Hope Publishing Company for "My Saviour First of All" by Fanny J. Crosby; to The Tabernacle Publishing Company for "When the Mists Have Rolled Away" by Annie Herbert; to the Sword of the Lord Publishers for quotations from "Eternal Retribution" by William Elbert Munsey.

CONTENTS

1

HELL IS NO JOKE

There was a certain rich man, which was clothed in purple and fine linen, and fared sumptuously every day:

And there was a certain beggar named Lazarus, which was laid at his gate, full of sores,

And desiring to be fed with the crumbs which fell from the rich man's table: moreover the dogs came and licked his sores.

And it came to pass, that the beggar died, and was carried by the angels into Abraham's bosom: the rich man also died, and was buried;

And in hell he lift up his eyes, being in torments, and seeth Abraham afar off, and Lazarus in his bosom.

And he cried and said, Father Abraham, have mercy on me, and send Lazarus, that he may dip the tip of his finger in water, and cool my tongue; for I am tormented in this flame.

But Abraham said, Son, remember that thou in thy lifetime receivedst thy good things, and likewise Lazarus evil things: but now he is comforted, and thou art tormented.

And beside all this, between us and you there is a great gulf fixed: so that they which would pass from hence to you cannot; neither can they pass to us, that would come from thence.

Then he said, I pray thee therefore, father, that thou wouldest send him to my father's house:

For I have five brethren; that he may testify unto them, lest they also come into this place of torment.

Abraham saith unto him, They have Moses and the prophets; let them hear them.

And he said, Nay, father Abraham: but if one went unto them from the dead, they will repent.

And he said unto him, If they hear not Moses and the prophets, neither will they be persuaded, though one rose from the dead (Luke 16:19-31).

7

Hell has long been riding high as the number one selection on the jokester "Hit Parade." More jokes are told, perhaps, with the Lake of Fire as their theme than with reference to any other single subject. Usually they feature the devil in long, red flannel underwear, cloven hooves, horns and a pitchfork tail. Mingled into the narrative are asbestos suits, Satan giving orders about how fast to shovel coal, and other incidental, colorful sidelights. The stories are usually climaxed with a rib-splitting punchline and followed by gales of laughter. Each one who joins in the ribaldry is subtly saying, consciously or unconsciously, "Yes, I think this business of Hell is just a great big joke! Surely it isn't anything to get seriously alarmed or excited about." But that philosophy is completely false! Hell *is* something to soberly, seriously consider with reference to its reality.

Hell is no joke! Consider what our Lord Jesus Christ, the highest authority in the universe about any matter, had to say in the above text about Hell! Note carefully His language about this home of eternal torment:

Jesus said in verse 23, "And in hell he lift up his eyes, being in torments . . ." In verse 24 the man in Hell cried out, ". . . I am tormented in this flame."

Abraham urged the rich man in Hell to remember what his life on earth had been like and to consider how the situation with reference to Lazarus and himself had been reversed. He said in verse 25, ". . . but now he is comforted, and thou art tormented."

In verse 28 the rich man in Hell is quoted by the Saviour as pleading for someone to go to his brothers and get them saved, ". . . lest they also come into this place of torment."

Make no mistake about it, Hell is a land of unspeakable and eternal torments! If God sends you to Hell it will not be to purify you, not to purge out any sin, not to salvage you or fit you for Heaven — but to damn you forever for your wicked sin in the rejection of His lovely Son, the Lord Jesus Christ. Hell certainly is not a playground, not a summer resort, not a reform or a remodeling school; it is a place of torment. If you think this is unjust you simply do not know or understand the horribleness of sin or the heinousness of rejecting Jesus Christ. Proverbs 28:5 says, "Evil men understand not judgment," but nevertheless, if you shut God out of your heart in this life, He will shut you out of His Heaven in the life to come. Dear sinner friend, as you read this Bible message about what Hell is really like, try to visualize yourself there in that land of torment forever unless you receive the Lord Jesus Christ as your own personal Saviour.

But the message of Hell is not for lost sinners alone! How profitable it would be if we could charter some New York Central trains or a fleet of Greyhound buses to take the Christians of our churches to that region of the damned for a tour through its corridors of horror. I assure you they would never be the same again and that it would make passionate, tireless, broken-hearted seekers of souls out of each one.

Years ago, when I was just a young preacher, the pages of *The Sword of the Lord* carried a message by that anointed pastor of the Moody Memorial Church, now in Heaven, Dr. H. A. Ironside. The sermon, on the same text as this one, was titled, "A Missionary-Minded Man in Hell!" How shocked I was at the subject; yet when I read the Scripture I was compelled to confess its truthfulness. I do not now recall a single point of his message or even one illustration he used, but that title has stayed with me and I never preach from this text without thinking of it. Yes, this ungodly man *was* missionary-minded after he woke up in Hell! He *was* concerned about soul-winning about revival, about evangelism, and especially about the winning of his own loved ones to the Saviour. Oh, if five minutes in Hell would do that for him, what would it do for our ministers, deacons, stewards, elders, Sunday school teachers, trustees and the ordinary men, women and young people of our Bible-believing churches?

Of course we cannot charter New York Central trains or Greyhound buses for such an excursion through the place God originally prepared for the devil and his angels. Even if we could, it would not be possible to return since there is no way out of that place of the damned once it has been entered. On the other hand, we can do the next best thing and show you plainly what the Word of God teaches about Hell, giving you some Scriptural word pictures of its eternal scenes of horror and woe.

Let me say first, however, that it is not my intention in this message to endeavor to prove the reality of Hell. I simply set it forth as a plain statement of Scriptural fact taught by no less an authority than the Saviour Himself. If you will not accept

His testimony and evidence there is nothing that I or anyone else has to offer which would convince you. When the rich man in Hell begged Abraham to send Lazarus or some other evangelist to his five brothers still on earth to warn them of their need for repentance, Abraham told him, "They have Moses and the prophets: let them hear them." In other words, he reminded him that his brothers had access to the Word of God and that they could read their Scriptures. When the rich man persisted, "Nay, father Abraham: but if one went unto them from the dead, they will repent," Abraham replied, "If they hear not Moses and the prophets, neither will they be persuaded though one rose from the dead." Folks who will not accept the testimony of the Bible would not even accept the evidence of a person who had come back from the dead with the story of an eternal torment to miss and the glory of a Heaven to gain through repentance and faith in Christ.

If you do not accept the testimony of the Word of God you would not believe even if an angel came to stand by your bed at three o'clock in the morning, aroused you from your slumber, then told you he had been sent from the throne of God to warn you of your need of Christ and urge you to repent. Instead of repenting, you would mentally rebuke yourself for eating apple pie and cheese just before retiring, roll over, go back to sleep, and the next morning tell your friends about the terrible nightmare you had. *You would not believe it!*

If you will not accept the testimony of the Word of God about Hell you would not be convinced of its reality even if some loved one — such as a gentle mother who had long been dead — suddenly appeared at your door and informed you that God had sent her back to warn you of the torments of Hell and urge you to trust in Jesus Christ. You would accuse others of finding a picture of your departed loved one, getting someone about the same height and build made up by an expert make-up artist so they could imitate that one, then trying to trick you into believing it was your loved one come back with a message. *No, you would not believe even if someone came back from the dead!*

Alfred Lord Tennyson, in the work for which he is probably best known of all, *In Memoriam*, commented that if his dear friend Arthur H. Hallam were to come back from the dead, he would not believe it. He went on to say that if Hallam appealed to incidents that had happened about which they alone were familiar, even making definite reference to past experiences, he would attribute it to mere human imagination playing tricks with his memory. His exact expression was:

> If any vision should reveal
> Thy likeness, I might count it vain
> As but the canker of the brain;
> Yea, though it spake and made appeal
>
> To chances where our lots were cast
> Together in the days behind,
> I might but say, I hear a wind
> Of memory murmuring the past.

Perhaps you will recall that after Herod beheaded John the Baptist and the ministry of the Lord Jesus came to his attention, his haunting conscience convinced him that it was John returned from the dead. But did he repent? *He did not!* He went right on with his sin and spurned every gospel appeal which came his way. Neither would you repent if you were convinced that someone had come back from the dead with a message of warning *if you will not accept the testimony of the Bible as it is!*

Suffice it to say that Hell is an awful but literal reality. Those who spurn the Saviour's love in salvation will learn with horror the truthfulness of such Scriptural statements as "For the Lord thy God is a consuming fire, even a jealous God" (Deut. 4:24), and, "It is a fearful thing to fall into the hands of the living God" (Heb. 10:31). *Hell is no joke!* In thinking of the terrible torments of this land of the lost, let us first consider

I. THE TORMENT OF ASSOCIATION FOREVER WITH THE WICKED

Hell is a place where the lost will make their abode with the vile of all ages including Satan, the demons, the fallen angels, the Antichrist and his false prophet, the Hitlers, the Mussolinis, the Stalins, the John Dilingers, the Al Capones, the Carl Austin Halls and Bonnie Headys, the Judas Iscariots, the harlots, drunkards, atheists, convicts, idolators and all other perverts of society.

For example, the Antichrist and his false prophet will be among the bedfellows of those in Hell. Revelation 19:20, looking down to the close of the Great Tribulation period, says about them, "These both were cast alive into a lake of fire burning with brimstone." The Antichrist and his false prophet will be there!

Revelation 20:10, referring to a time following Christ's millennial reign on earth, says, "And the devil that deceived them was cast into the lake of fire and brimstone, where the beast and the false prophet are, and shall be tormented day and night for ever and ever." Satan will be a companion of the inhabitants of Hell! Note here also that he will not be a boss issuing orders to others, but he will be confined and tormented just as any other sinner. As a matter of fact, he will be tormented much more than any other since he is the greatest sinner deserving the greatest punishment for his iniquity. It is also interesting to observe from this verse of Scripture that Satan is not yet in Hell and when he is sent there it will be on a one-way ticket. Hell is not Satan's office of operations today from which he runs back and forth to trouble the inhabitants of earth, as some so foolishly imagine.

The fallen angels will also be the companions of the lost. II Peter 2:4 says, "God spared not the angels that sinned, but cast them down to hell, and delivered them into chains of darkness, to be reserved unto judgment." The fallen angels will be there!

All the vilest of the vile will be the associates of every Christ-rejecting sinner for ever. Revelation 21:8 describes it, "But the fearful, and unbelieving, and the abominable, and murderers, and whoremongers, and sorcerers, and idolaters, and all liars, shall have their part in the lake which burneth with fire and brimstone: which is the second death." The chapter goes on to give a beautiful description of Heaven, at the close of which it says, "And there shall in no wise enter into it anything that defileth, neither whatsoever worketh abomination, or maketh a lie: but they which are written in the Lamb's book of life" (Rev. 21:27). Since those who defile, work abomination, and make lies will not be allowed entrance into Heaven, there is only one other place for them to go and that is into the eternal Hell.

It says the same thing in the twenty-second chapter of Revelation where, after another glorious description of Heaven, we read in verse 15: "For without are dogs, and sorcerers, and whoremongers, and murderers, and idolaters, and whosoever loveth and maketh a lie." Hell is a land where the lost rub shoulders with whoremongers, murderers, sorcerers, idolaters, the abominable, the unbelieving, and all other defilers of themselves with mankind. Any individual with refined sensibilities would abhor the thought of spending eternity with such a motley crowd. Surely for them it would be torment!

Dr. Robert P. Shuler, who during the third of a century he ministered at Los Angeles' Trinity Methodist Church earned for himself the title of "Fighting Bob," tells of an incident which took place when he was just a boy preacher down in Pocahontas, Virginia. Late one afternoon he received a call to go to a certain address and talk with a dying girl. Recognizing the location as being right in the heart of the little mining town's red light district, he hesitated until the woman informed him the girl could not live through the night and had been calling for a Methodist minister to tell her how she could be saved. It was the type of appeal he could not refuse and so he asked an elderly man of about eighty to accompany him. His granddaughter played the organ in the Methodist chapel every Sunday night.

It was about dusk when they walked down the boardwalk of that town which saw murders every payday and abounded in vices of every possible description. Women were already standing in the doors of their rooms and cribs encouraging the men to come in. Shuler said he saw a white woman and a Negro man, arms entwined about each other, come staggering down the street. It was the first white woman he had seen drunk in his life. Sin and iniquity abounded on every side in a most sickening manner.

Finding the address, they went in to talk with a beautiful but wasted girl in her early twenties. She told them a tragic tale of grievous sin — betrayed by a lover, disowned by her mother, then tobogganing downward until she found herself in her present position. She tearfully stated her fear that she had gone so far in sin God no longer loved her and it was impossible to be saved. They told her about the woman of John 8 who was caught in the act of adultery and how Jesus forgave her. They told her about the woman at the well of Sychar who had had many husbands and was living in open sin at the very time she was converted. They told her about Mary Magdalene, out of whom Jesus had cast seven demons. They told her how the blasphemous dying thief had been converted when he had one foot in Hell, so to speak. They quoted the many "whosoever wills" in the Word of God. Finally she was assured the Saviour would forgive even such as she and happily put her faith and trust in Him.

After some further counseling and prayer, the men left and started homeward back through the heart of the town. The scene of iniquity which had so nauseated them before was multiplied many times over. Striding the second time that night past the sickening sights of sin all about them, Shuler turned to his elderly companion and said, "Did you ever think about your beautiful sixteen-year-old granddaughter living and associating with this kind of crowd?"

The nonplussed old man stopped dead in his tracks, faced Shuler with fighting fury written all over his ashen countenance turned pale with anger, doubled up his fists and spat at him through clenched teeth, "Just what do you mean by that?"

The young preacher replied, "I simply mean that I talked with her only this past week and she has never yet made her great decision in favor of Jesus Christ. Nor would she settle it when I talked to her. If I understand my Bible aright, this is the kind of companionship she will have forever unless she repents."

The old man simply stood looking at the minister several moments, then without a word started walking briskly up the boardwalk again. They came to his residence and the old man walked through the wicket gate, up the steps and into the house without so much as a "Good night." But he had gotten the vision I hope every Christian who reads these lines will get: he saw his lovely granddaughter in the torment of association with the wicked forever unless she turned to Christ.

The next Sunday night after Shuler preached a simple gospel message, by prearrangement someone else played the organ during the invitation and the old man walked over to his granddaughter, took her by the hand and brought her down the aisle in an open, public profession of faith in Jesus Christ.

Oh, the awfulness of Hell and its association with the unredeemed and the unrepentant! If you die unsaved you will wallow in eternity's garbage pile forever. The Lord Jesus Christ repeatedly used the Valley of Hinnom, or Gehenna — just outside the dung gate of the city of Jerusalem — as an illustration of Hell. There the rubbish and debris of the city was dumped and burned with a fire which never went out. *Hell is like that!*

Next, think with me of

II. THE TORMENT OF ETERNAL SEPARATION FROM LOVED ONES

In Luke 13:28 the Saviour told the unsaved religious leaders of His time, "There shall be weeping and gnashing of teeth, when ye shall see Abraham, and Isaac, and Jacob, and all the prophets, in the kingdom of God, and you yourselves thrust out."

People of that day did not think about Heaven as we do today in terms of reunion with some loved one who has gone on before, such as a Christian mother, a godly dad, or a baby who died in infancy. Nor did they think about Heaven in terms of a place of fellowship with a Saviour who had died for them on the Cross. Instead, Heaven was a wonderful land of opportunity to be forever with the fathers of their nation. How they longed to be with Abraham, Isaac, Jacob, Moses, Daniel, Isaiah and other prophets of the Old Testament victories! Jesus was simply saying to them, "There will be weeping and wailing when you see those whom you most want to be with enter into Heaven and you yourselves be thrust out."

What terrible torment it will be for you, as one who has turned down Jesus Christ, to be eternally separated from your Christian friends and loved ones. It means you will never again feel the tender touch of a loving mother or experience the sweet caress of a devoted mate. I read recently of a couple in Idaho who celebrated their eightieth wedding anniversary on Thanksgiving Day. Think of it, eighty years of happy wedded union! A few days later — the day after Christmas to be exact — the husband stepped out into eternity, leaving behind his widow, three sons, fifteen grandchildren, fifty-one great-grandchildren and fifty-one great-great-grandchildren.

I do not know anything, of course, about the spiritual relationship of that couple before God. However, since such is often the case, let us suppose one was saved and the other lost. It would mean that after eighty years of wedded sweetness and fellowship they are to be separated eternally. After eighty years

of wedded companionship and communion, one would step out
into Heaven and the other out into Hell. Many couples are married fifty years or more and never separated a single night, yet
will be banished from each other's presence for eternity because of the failure of one to be saved.

There are several songs which always stir my heart when-
ever I hear them sung. For example, there is the song, "Tell
Mother I'll Be There." But you will not be there because you
turned down mother's God and refused to be saved! There is
a song, "Where Is My Wandering Boy Tonight?" But you, the
wandering boy, will be in Hell, never again to see mother's
sweet face or hear her praying voice. Oh, the terrible torment
of eternal separation from redeemed loved ones!

But that is not all! If you die without Christ and sink
out into this Bible Hell you will experience separation from
even your unsaved loved ones. By that I mean you will not
enjoy fellowship or companionship with them as you have known
it in this life. I remember speaking several years ago in the city
of Sacramento, California, from the text in Amos 4:12, "Prepare to meet thy God." It was early in 1946, right after World
War II. I explained that a preparation must be made for meeting God and that the only acceptable preparation is to experience a new birth through faith in the Lord Jesus Christ.

As I stressed the importance of forgiveness of sins and the
absolute necessity of this new birth, suddenly a young man
about fifteen years of age who was sitting on the front row
stood to his feet and said, "Brother Sumner, I had a brother
twenty-two years old who fell mortally wounded at the Normandy beachhead. He had never been born again. He had
never trusted in Christ. Do you mean to tell me that he is in
Hell even though he made the supreme sacrifice and gave his
life for his country?"

Not only for his benefit, of course, but for the others present
I was compelled to speak the truth according to the Scripture.
I said, "Son, the Bible says in Romans 3:22 and 23, '. . . for there
is no difference: For all have sinned, and come short of the
glory of God.' There is no difference in the fact of sin. There
is no difference in the way of salvation. The gate of Heaven
does not swing open to receive one for giving his life for his
country, to another for rescuing a baby from a burning build-

ing, to another for giving great donations to charity, and to still another for putting his faith and trust in Jesus Christ. The only way into Heaven is by faith in the Son of God. However, you do not know that your brother died without Christ. Perhaps some godly chaplain called his men together that night as they neared the beachhead and said, 'Men, this is it. As we approach the zero hour we know some of us will be in eternity before the dawning of another day. Let me tell you how you can enter Heaven as soon as you leave this life,' and won your brother to Jesus. Or perhaps some buddy who had been with him through basic slipped up to him on the boat, put his arm around his shoulder and said, 'Fellow, if the bullet has my number on it, I am ready to go. My faith is in Jesus Christ and Him crucified. But if it has your number on it, you are not ready. Won't you trust the Lord Jesus Christ as your personal Saviour? God loves you, Christ died for you, and you can be saved by faith,' and led him to Christ. You do not know that your brother died lost. Perhaps he is in Heaven right now!"

As long as I live I will not forget that lad's bitter reply as he said to me, "No, I *know* that he died unsaved, a Christ-rejector. And if my brother is in Hell, I want to go to Hell to be with him!"

As he dropped tearfully but defiantly into his seat, I said, "Son, you just don't understand what Hell is like. If you go to Hell and your brother is there, you will have no loving companionship, no sweet fellowship with him such as you experienced on this earth."

That is true! Those who die lost are not only eternally separated from redeemed loved ones, but from unredeemed loved ones as well.

The reason for this is seen in the next torment I must mention,

III. THE TORMENT OF ETERNAL DARKNESS IN HELL

Hell is a land of midnight blackness and darkness so thick it can be felt. In the verse already quoted about fallen angels, II Peter 2:4, their fate is described as being "delivered . . . into chains of darkness." The seventeenth verse of that same chapter, referring this time to unconverted preachers, says, ". . . to whom the mist of darkness is reserved for ever."

In Jude 13, also speaking of false prophets and unsaved

preachers, we read, ". . . to whom is reserved the blackness of darkness for ever." This agrees with what our Lord said in Matthew 8:12: "But the children of the kingdom shall be cast out into outer darkness: there shall be weeping and gnashing of teeth." Hell is thus described as a place of "chains of darkness," "mist of darkness," "blackness of darkness," and "outer darkness."

Can you visualize being in a place of such eternal darkness, a place where the rays of the sun never pierce, where the twinkle of the stars and the luster of the moon never reach? Can you imagine a land where no one can walk into a room, flip a switch and flood that room with electric light? Can you imagine a place where the sun never rises and day never comes — it is only night forever? If you can visualize this you have realized merely one of the awful torments of an eternal Hell. How tragic it will be if the Saviour is compelled to say of you, "Bind him hand and foot, and take him away, and cast him into outer darkness; there shall be weeping and gnashing of teeth" (Matt. 22:13).

I remember hearing the noted evangelist and university founder, Bob Jones, tell of a lady who had trained her pet parrot to say "Good night" and "Good morning." Each evening she would place the cloth covering over the parrot's cage and say, "Good night, Polly," and the parrot would respond, "Good night." In the morning as she lifted the cover off the cage she would say, "Good morning, Polly," and the parrot would say, "Good morning."

One day the parrot escaped from his cage momentarily and before it was discovered he got into a fight with the family cat. That night when his mistress covered his cage and said, "Good night, Polly," he immediately responded with the usual, "Good night." However, when she lifted the cloth from the cage the following day and said, "Good morning, Polly," the parrot replied, "Good night." Shocked at his mistake, she replied again, "Good morning, Polly," only to have him reply the second time, "Good night." Closer examination revealed the parrot's eyes had been scratched out the day before in the fight with the cat and Polly would never again know "Good morning" — only "Good night."

Hell is an eternal "Good night" for every sinner who leaves

this life without Christ. Never again will he have a "Good morning" since the sun never rises in that land of anguish and despair. What a terrible thing it is to be lost!

Less than a dozen miles from where I was born there is one of the most unusual graves in the world. I have a picture of it in my study. It is not expensive, elaborate or fancy, but it is highly unusual. It seems that a boy of about fourteen or fifteen — whose father did not have any time for God or religion — lay dying. In the boy's ignorance of what death was really like he had a terrible fear of the grave. From the few funerals he had attended he supposed that when he died they would take him to the cemetery, a hole would be dug, he would be lowered into the ground, the dirt would be thrown over him, and the darkness of the grave would be most terrifying. He did not know, of course, that the very moment an individual dies the spirit and soul leave the body and enter immediately into Heaven or Hell. He did not understand that it is just the earthly tabernacle of dust in which the real person lived during his lifetime that is placed in a cemetery grave. But because of his fear of darkness he begged his daddy with his dying breath to put a window in his grave to let the sunlight in.

The ungodly daddy, with tears streaming down his face, clutched his boy's hand and promised that his grave would have a window. Today, if you should go to that small, unpretentious cemetery you would find a simple grave with an unusual shape. It has a mound built up several inches from the level ground. On the front of that mound, shaped somewhat like the top half of an octagon, are three thin stones. The center stone, which is flush up against the mound, has a glass window in the center to let the sunlight down to where the casket rests. The daddy kept his vow and the boy's grave has a window.

The lad in his ignorance of the Bible did not understand what happens at death, but he did grasp a portion of Scriptural truth unwittingly. The very moment an individual dies he *does* enter into a place of blackness and darkness far more terrifying than the mere darkness of a cemetery grave. If he leaves this life without Jesus Christ as personal Saviour, he steps into the "mist of blackness and darkness" of eternal Hell. The lost person goes at once to a place where neither friend nor foe can fashion a window allowing the light to penetrate. How tormenting must be that place of eternal darkness!

The reason for this torment of darkness in Hell is explained by the next horror we will consider,

IV. THE TORMENT OF ETERNAL DEATH IN HELL

Did you know death and Hell are associated together several times in sacred Scripture? For example, in Revelation 1:18, Jesus said, "I am he that liveth, and was dead; and, behold, I am alive for evermore, Amen; and have the keys of hell and of death." In Revelation 20:13, 14, speaking of the Great Judgment Morning, the Word of God says, "And the sea gave up the dead which were in it; and death and hell delivered up the dead which were in them: and they were judged every man according to their works. And death and hell were cast into the lake of fire. This is the second death."

Death, remember, is simply separation. When an individual dies the soul and the spirit are separated from his body. Because we do not know how else to describe that separation, we say that one is "dead." In like manner the Bible describes the condition of lost people as "dead in trespasses and sins" (Eph. 2:1). Because of their separation from God they are considered "dead." If they continue through life rejecting Jesus Christ, dying physically in that spiritually dead state, they will be eternally, completely, finally separated from God. The Scripture calls this "the second death"!

Hebrews 2:9 speaks of the Lord's death on the Cross and comments that "he by the grace of God should taste death for every man." In what sense did Jesus taste death for every man? It could not refer to physical death since every man tastes that for himself — even those who put their faith and trust in Jesus Christ. For centuries past saints have personally walked down into "the valley of the shadow of death," and they will continue doing so until Christ comes again.

The explanation of how He tasted death for all is seen in His cry on the Cross: "And at the ninth hour Jesus cried with a loud voice, saying, Eloi, Eloi, lama sabachthani? which is, being interpreted, My God, my God, why hast thou forsaken me?" (Mark 15:34). Since Jesus Christ at Calvary was tasting the torments of Hell for sinners it was absolutely necessary He be forsaken of the Father and that the eternal fellowship that He, as Son, had enjoyed with the Father be broken off. If He was to take our punishment He must experience that being forsaken and separated from God which our sin deserved. He did taste that death for us and now we need not experience it if only we will accept Him as our personal Saviour and sin-bearer. If we do not receive Him as our Saviour we must experience that separation, or "death," ourselves.

That is the meaning in II Thessalonians 1:7-9 when we read: "And to you who are troubled rest with us, when the Lord Jesus shall be revealed from heaven with his mighty angels, In flaming fire taking vengeance on them that know not God, and that obey not the gospel of our Lord Jesus Christ: Who shall be punished with everlasting destruction from the presence of the Lord, and from the glory of his power." Notice the Scripture says that those who refuse to be saved by obeying the Gospel of our Lord Jesus Christ will be punished with "everlasting destruction *from* the presence of the Lord, and *from* the glory of his power." The torment of death in Hell is to be separated from God and His glory.

Death in the Scripture *never* means annihilation or ceasing to exist! It simply refers to being completely and finally separated from Almighty God and everything which comes from Him. A sinner in this life is not completely separated from God in the sense that he receives many good and perfect things from His hand. For example, the Saviour said in Matthew 5:45 that the Father "maketh his sun to rise on the evil and on the good, and sendeth rain on the just and on the unjust." Lost people have many of the blessings of God in their lives and Romans 2:4 tells us that this "riches of his goodness and forbearance and longsuffering" is an endeavor on His part to lead them to repentance. However, if they do not repent before they die they must sink out into an eternal Hell where separation from God will be complete and final.

That is why there is no light in Hell, only blackness and darkness. The Scripture tells us "God is light" (I John 1:5), yet nothing that comes from God will penetrate the corridors of Hell. That is why there is no love in Hell for "God is love" (I John 4:16). There will be nothing good in Hell, nothing perfect, nothing of holiness, nothing of blessing, only that which has God's curse upon it. Men, women and young people who live without God, who by their lives say, "Jesus, I don't want you; I won't have you," will be cast from His presence forever. Oh, the terrible torment of death in Hell with its eternal separation from Almighty God! This, in my estimation, is by far the worst of all Hell's terrible torments.

Next, think with me of

V. THE TORMENT OF UNSPEAKABLE SORROW IN HELL

Hell is a land completely devoid of any joy whatsoever. No laughter is ever heard echoing down its corridors. No childish glee or youth's bright joy radiates in that land of night. Things that delight, that please, that thrill the soul are wiped forever from the consciousness of the doomed. Great grief reigns supreme without relief, reprieve or rest.

The Saviour emphasized this truth when He said in Matthew 13:41, 42, "The Son of man shall send forth his angels, and they shall gather out of his kingdom all things that offend, and them which do iniquity; And shall cast them into a furnace of fire: there shall be wailing and gnashing of teeth."

A little farther on in the same chapter, again emphasizing the fate of the forever lost, He said: "So shall it be at the end of the world: the angels shall come forth, and sever the wicked from among the just, And shall cast them into the furnace of fire: there shall be wailing and gnashing of teeth" (vv. 49, 50).

In Luke 13:28 He commented about the "weeping and gnashing of teeth." David spoke several times of the "sorrows of hell" (II Sam. 22:6; Ps. 18:5).

There is a Southern song about Heaven entitled, "Everybody Will Be Happy over There," but that certainly is not true of Hell. No one will be happy in Hell! Instead it will be a miserable land of weeping, wailing, cursing, bitterness, malice, gnashing of teeth and misery overflowing. What a horrible fog of gloom, grief and indescribable woe hangs over the chambers of that eternal night!

Next, there is

VI. THE TORMENT OF THE SCORPION-LIKE STING OF MEMORY AND THE BITTER, BITING, BURNING REMORSE OF A GNASHING, GNAWING, GUILTY CONSCIENCE

When the rich man in Hell asked for the moist fingertip of Lazarus to be placed on his feverish tongue, Abraham summed up his refusal by replying, "Son, remember . . . " In Daniel 12:2 we are told, "And many of them that sleep in the dust of the earth shall awake, some to everlasting life, and some to shame and everlasting contempt." There will be memory in Hell which will produce shame and continual contempt.

Memory is a horrible, haggarding, haunting thing: a tormenting Hell in itself. Here in the United States there are over a half-million suicide attempts every year — at least one attempt every minute around the clock, both night and day — and the reason for the majority is that their sins have found them out in their conscience and they seek to evade the torture of its blistering condemnation. Rather than face the music, they choose to jump off a high building or put a revolver to their temple and blow out their brains. But Hell is a land where men find it impossible to escape the shame and contempt of their sin. If there were no devil, no demons, no sinners, no ungodly associates, no darkness or sorrow in Hell, memory would be incentive sufficient for me to want to keep out, to miss it and gain Heaven. Yes, you will remember in Hell!

For one thing, you will remember every opportunity to accept the Lord Jesus Christ as your personal Saviour which you spurned. You will remember your mother's prayers, your friends' tearful pleas, the persistent warnings of those who were interested in your soul. You will remember every gospel message you ever heard or read. This particular message with its strong Biblical warning about the horrors of an everlasting Hell will haunt you forever because of the light manner in which you passed off its Scriptural plea.

The funeral dirge of Hell will be the sorrowful ballad, "It might have been!" Oh, to be so near salvation, so near the Kingdom of God, yet delay the decision until sudden death and its grim declaration of "no remedy" strikes eternal condemnation to your soul. You will have all eternity to regret your folly, your indecision, your failure to be saved. "Son, remember . . ."

You will also remember your sins in Hell. Most of your iniquities and transgressions have now long been forgotten by you, and just a few of the outstanding ones come to mind. But in Hell all the skeletons of your secret closets will come out to haunt you forever. With a quickened conscience and a perfect memory, the awful horror of your rebellion against the commands of righteousness and your eager submission to the subtle suggestions of Satan's devices will be a portion of your torment "unto the ages of the ages." Things now forgotten and erased by time will stand out just as boldly as the reality of the present hour. George Eliot, the master novelist, unwittingly portrayed a sample of the horror of Hell when she painted on the pages of her literature the picture of a young girl who sinned grievously, then murdered the babe born in her sin. In direct harmony with God's warning, "be sure your sin will find you out" (Num. 32:23), her terrible transgressions came to light. When a friendly woman tried to comfort her, she simply cried out despairingly over and over, "But will I always hear that cry?" In like manner, souls in Hell will be devoid of the slightest comfort as the echoes of their iniquities haunt them forever.

Down in Texas, a land notorious for its millionaires among the cattle barons and oil tycoons, there lived a man who had amassed a tremendous fortune by defrauding the poor, pulling shady business deals, misrepresenting facts, and otherwise hoodwinking the innocent and the ignorant. He eventually became one of the richest millionaires in the state, but he never reached the place where he could really enjoy his ill-gotten gain. Instead, as he grew older, the consciousness of his crimes weakened his mind until eventually relatives were compelled to confine him in a private mental institution. There in his padded cell he would pace the floor and cry out over and over, "This land, it is not mine! This money, it is not really my money! These cattle, they are not mine! These stocks and bonds, they are not really my stocks and bonds! Oh, that I didn't have a head of cattle, that I didn't own any stocks and bonds, that I didn't have a foot of land, that I didn't have a single oil well! They're not mine! *They're not mine!* THEY'RE NOT MINE!"

Could you imagine living for eternity with a conscience like that? Yet that is just one of the awful horrors of Hell to be experienced by every inhabitant of doom. No wonder it is called "Eternity's Madhouse" and "the Asylum of the Ages"! Another of Hell's horrors is centered around

VII. THE TORMENT OF UNSATISFIED LUSTFUL CRAVINGS

Do you realize that in Hell there will not be a single thing which will satisfy? I read a sermon some time ago by a preacher in Detroit who stated that there would be no sin in Hell. He was a noble, good, sincere man but he was mistaken in this instance. It will be necessary for you to go to Heaven to reach a place of sinless perfection! The character which you are developing in this life will live on and on in Hell forever. This is the meaning of the angel's message to John in Revelation 22:11, "He that is unjust, let him be unjust still: and he which is filthy, let him be filthy still: and he that is righteous, let him be righteous still: and he that is holy, let him be holy still." Unjust sinners who are cast into Hell will remain unjust forever. Filthy souls who neglected to come to Christ for cleansing in the blood of the Lamb will remain filthy forever in Hell. Possibly the American Standard Version brings the thought out even more clearly when it translates that verse, "He that is unrighteous, let him do unrighteousness still." The unrighteous will continue to do unrighteousness in Hell, the Bible says.

However, the Detroit pastor was partly right in the sense that the sinning of the damned in Hell will be limited to the lust of the heart and mind rather than the fulfillment of the deed in action and reality. Remember that sins of the heart are as wicked in the sight of God as the sins of action. We are told in Proverbs 24:9, "The thought of foolishness is sin . . ."

By way of illustration, the seventh commandment warns, "Thou shalt not commit adultery" (Ex. 20:14), but Jesus enlarged upon that truth when He said in Matthew 5:27, 28, "Ye have heard that it was said by them of old time, Thou shalt not commit adultery: But I say unto you, That whosoever looketh on a woman to lust after her hath committed adultery with her already in his heart." One is a sin of deed while the other is a sin of heart, but both alike are sin in the sight of a holy God.

In like manner the sixth commandment warns us, "Thou shalt not kill" (Ex. 20:13), but John enlarged upon that injunction when he wrote, "Whosoever hateth his brother is a murderer . . ." (I John 3:15). One is a sin of action, the other is a sin of thought.

Suffice it to say that Hell is a land where passions run wild but are never gratified. The appetites you feed now will cry unsuccessfully for appeasement throughout all eternity. Have you ever seen a dope fiend crying for his narcotic when his body needs another shot? His eyes have a wild, fierce look, bulging far out of the sockets. He looks and acts like a crazy man. He *is* a crazy man: a man out of his mind. He will lie, steal, kill or do anything else to get the money to buy dope or to get the dope itself. In Hell the dope fiend will not have his dope, just the eternal longing and desiring for it cultivated in time. All appetites will bring exactly the same reaction in Hell whether they be for dope, tobacco, liquor, lust or some other lesser sin in the eyes of the finite. As another has already suggested, Hell is a place where the Belshazzars will not have their wine, where the Ahabs will not have their Naboth's vineyards, where the Felixes will not have their Drusillas, where the Herods will not have their sensuous dances, and where the Judases will not have their cankered gold.

I have in my home a picture of a fifty-year-old merchant marine commander and his forty-seven-year-old wife. They owned a lovely home on fashionable Rice Boulevard in Houston, Texas. On one occasion neighbors thought they had left the city since all the Venetian blinds were drawn, newspapers and milk bottles were piled on the front porch, the hedges and lawn were uncared for, and other evidences pointed to an empty house.

Then one night about two months later the neighbors heard suspicious noises coming from the inside of the house and phoned the West University Police Chief, Captain Grady Smith. Smith came out immediately with two of his men, walked around the house, tried to see inside through the windows but couldn't because of the drawn blinds, so returned to his squad car and phoned for a hook and ladder. He had the firemen run a ladder up to a second story window, crawled up himself to look in, failed to see anything, so came down the ladder and went to one of the rear doors. Taking his revolver from its holster, he used the handle to smash the glass, reached in and unsnapped the nightlock, opened the door and walked into the house. A tremendous mess of dirt and debris greeted his eyes. Bottles and garbage were everywhere. Going into the living room he found the marine commander, completely unclothed, crawling across the floor with a broken chair leg in his hand. He was mumbling, "Forward, men, forward! We've got to take this beachhead!" He was hopelessly intoxicated.

Going upstairs — in the only clean room in the house, a bedroom — Smith found the commander's wife kneeling beside her bed in a praying position. Her arms were folded on the bed and her head was resting on her arms. She had been dead about four hours. They rushed the commander to the hospital but he died within two hours after arriving. Justice of the Peace Thomas Mays ruled that death in both cases was due to acute alcoholism.

Police investigation uncovered evidence showing that for two months friends had been bringing in what little food they had eaten and a taxi driver had delivered whisky daily. Over 200 empty whisky bottles were found scattered throughout the house in closets, sink, commode, bathtub, chairs and every other conceivable place. Drinking an average of three or four bottles of whisky a day for sixty straight days, they had literally drunk themselves to death.

Poor, poor, lost, deceived, blinded souls! There will be no beer, no wine, no whisky, no gin, no brandy or other forms of alcoholic beverage in Hell. Imagine the tormenting craving of one who has developed a passion for liquor in this life as he is denied the fulfillment of that desire in Hell! What horror it will be to have an insatiable longing in the heart for sin, yet denied the gratification. Such a torment has been described in Joel 1:5, "Awake, ye drunkards, and weep; and howl, all ye drinkers of wine, because of the new wine; for it is cut off from your mouth." There will be weeping and howling in Hell when those who have developed a passion and appetite for drink have it cut off from their mouths forever.

But such torment will not be limited to liquor lovers alone; every sin will find a kindred reaction. Hell is a home of horror

where the lustful cravings of the lost are never satisfied but
the longings burn on in the breast eternally.

Another feature in the agony of the damned is described by

VIII. THE TORMENT OF DESPAIR IN HELL — No HOPE, DOOMED FOREVER

In our text Abraham reminded the rich man in Hell, "And
beside all this, between us and you there is a great gulf fixed:
so that they which would pass from hence to you cannot;
neither can they pass to us, that would come from thence"
(Luke 16:26). Hell has a great gulf fixed which makes it impossible for any who enter that land of despair to ever return.
Transgressors riding the express train of sin into Hell have a
one-way ticket.

The Saviour said in Matthew 25:41, "Then shall he say also
unto them on the left hand, Depart from me, ye cursed, into
everlasting fire, prepared for the devil and his angels." Note
that the Son of God referred to the torments of Hell as "everlasting fire." He went on to say in the same chapter, "And
these shall go away into everlasting punishment: but the righteous into life eternal" (v. 46). The punishment and torment
of Hell lasts for ever; it is "everlasting punishment."

Revelation 14:10, 11 describes the eternal endlessness of horror for the lost with the words: "The same shall drink of the
wine of the wrath of God, which is poured out without mixture
into the cup of his indignation; and he shall be tormented with
fire and brimstone in the presence of the holy angels, and in
the presence of the Lamb: And the smoke of their torment
ascendeth up for ever and ever: and they have no rest day
nor night. . . ."

The words here translated, "for ever and ever," are literally
"unto the ages of the ages." In Ephesians 2:7 the same duration of time is mentioned about the joys of eternity in Heaven
for the redeemed. The horrors of Hell cannot, *will not* cease
any sooner than the joys of Heaven; both are eternal.

Can you imagine how awful it will be to have hope forever
gone? Though not a Christian, Bernard M. Baruch called "hopeless" the saddest word in the English language and he was not
far wrong. What would you do if robbed of hope? In our age
we live by hope. If we are sick, we hope we will get better.

If business is bad, we hope it will improve. If things are gloomy, we hope something will happen before long to cheer us up. Even the inmates of a penitentiary's death row, awaiting the hour of their execution, live by hope and seek to fan its faint glimmer in their souls with the pleasant thought that perhaps there will be a pardon, a reprieve, or even a stay of execution before the fatal hour arrives. *But in Hell hope is forever gone!* There is nothing there to look forward to on the part of the lost but eternal torment, darkness, despair and doom. There are no exits in Hell and whoever goes in must remain forever. He can never come out again! As Dante inscribed over the door of his Inferno, "Ye who enter here leave all hope behind."

No one can even begin to fathom the height, depth, length or breadth of eternity! Gibbons well expressed it for us all when he wrote those lines of wisdom:

> What is *eternity?* can aught
> Paint its duration to the thought?
> Tell all the sand the ocean laves,
> Tell all its changes, all its waves,
> Or, tell with more laborious pains,
> The drops its mighty mass contains;
> Be this astonishing account
> Augmented with the full amount
> Of all the drops that clouds have shed,
> Where'er their wat'ry fleeces spread,
> Through all time's long protracted tour,
> From Adam to the present hour;—
> Still short the sum, nor can it vie
> With the more numerous years that lie
> Embossed in *eternity*.
> Attend, O man, with awe divine,
> For this *eternity* is thine.

The old-time Methodist minister, William Elbert Munsey, wrote of this despair:

Eternity is an infinite line. The strongest winged angel who cleaves the illimitable ether may track it, and track it forever, yet he can no more find its end than he can find the cradle or tomb of God. The plodding and incarnated soul of man can find it just as quickly. It is a day without a morning, a day without an evening — an eternal noon. It was just noon when the world was made, it will be just noon when the world is destroyed — high noon forever. O Eternity! The idea deepens, widens, and towers, till the human mind, confounded and crushed, shrinks into infinite littleness, and frightened flies into its temple, closes all the doors, and tries to hide its little self forever.

. . . O Eternity! Mother of cycles, and parent of ages, whose incalculable and incomprehensible value no substraction can diminish, no addition increase — thou only type of deity, and day of His duration — what must be thy significance when joined to the stern penalty of sin thou becomest to the lost *Eternal Death*. Dreadful phrase! It will be written with a fiery pen upon all the walls of Hell, and seared into every arch by the lightning's blaze, and sounded through every dungeon by the thunder's horrid breath. It is the motto upon the seal of God which fastens the doors of woe. There are no farewells in Heaven. Such a word never rang in chords of breaking anguish from the harps of the redeemed, or shrieked in their harmonious preludes, or danced upon their vibrating strings — also, there are no farewells in Hell — O Eternity! Eternity!!

Again, this fiery Methodist orator wrote:

O Eternity! let thy ages tramp, thy cycles roll, but thou canst not crumble or scar the walls of Hell, or rust and break its locks or silver the hair of God, who has sworn by His eternal self that the sinner shall die. The pendulum of thy horologe over the gates of woe vibrates through all aeons, and says, "forever, and ever" — "forever, and ever" — "forever and ever" — its sounding bell striking off the centuries, the ages — the cycles. The appalling monotony of its pendulum — going — going — going — repeating still, "forever, and ever" — "forever and ever," — "forever and ever" — O Eternity! God has wound up thy clock and it will never run down — and its tickings and beatings are heard by all the lost — "forever and ever" — "forever and ever" — "forever and ever." God being my judge, I would die to save you this day.

Isaiah 38:18 describes it this way, "For the grave cannot praise thee, death cannot celebrate thee: they that go down into the pit cannot hope for thy truth." Note that those who sink down into the pit of Hell "cannot hope" for God's truth. Proverbs 11:7 enlarges on this fact when it says frankly, "When a wicked man dieth, his expectation shall perish: and the hope of unjust men perisheth." The very moment a lost man dies his expectation is gone eternally and his hope has forever perished. The lost person cannot ever "hope" to get out of Hell.

Some time ago the *Detroit News* printed a humorous note which was entitled, "Leaves Hell for Paradise!" The article told of a State Conservation Department employee named Harold Peterson who "moved from Hell to Paradise." It seems

that Peterson was a park ranger at the Pinckney Recreation Area
and lived in a little community once known as Hell. When the
Conservation Department transferred him to the Tahquamenon
Falls Park he moved into a little near-by hamlet of about
seventy-five population, called Paradise. The Associated Press
dispatch jokingly remarked that since his present job was farther
north Peterson was "afraid winters are going to be a little
colder" and noted that "the Conservation Department said it
was a good move and Peterson got a raise in pay." But the
real Hell is a land from which no one is transferred into Paradise. Once in means in forever!

In the July, 1952, issue of the *Reader's Digest*, I read a fas-
cinating article entitled, "The Case of Willie Sutton." It seems
Sutton was an escape artist who boasted that no penitentiary
or jail in the land could hold him. They sent him to the
Holmesburg Prison in Pennsylvania, one thought to be escape-
proof and called by authorities "the Alcatraz of Pennsylvania."
Exactly one year and four months after his confinement at
Holmesburg, Sutton and two of his companions went over the
wall. But there will be no inmate able to go over the wall in
Hell! Once in, never out! The Willie Suttons will remain con-
fined in Hell forever.

The same article told of an escape from Eastern State Penitentiary in Philadelphia. A prisoner was leaning against the
wall in his cell one day when a large rock fell out of the wall.
Looking into the opening he discovered that his cell block had
been built next to another, but the authorities had left an
opening about two feet wide between the two buildings. Crawling into the opening, the inmate went to the end of the passage
and found it led almost to the outside wall of the prison. He
put the rock back into place and the next day he stole a tablespoon from the dining hall. Immediately he and the others in
his cell began digging a tablespoon of dirt a night, putting the
dirt into their pockets and brushing it out on the parade ground
the next day or flushing it down the commode that night. Slowly
they worked on, tablespoon by tablespoon, day after day, week
after week, month after month, for over a year until they had
dug a little tunnel underneath the wall and had escaped to
liberty on the outside. But Hell is a land where sinners could
tunnel for billions of years with the most efficient bulldozers,

caterpillars, steam shovels and every modernized, mechanized type of machinery, yet never tunnel their way out. Dear reader, listen to the Holy Scripture as it states the truth that *there is no way out of Hell!* Here is the horror of being confined in that madhouse with hope of a pardon or eventual release forever gone!

Think with me also of

IX. THE TORMENT OF THE UNQUENCHABLE FLAME OF BRIMSTONE AND FIRE IN HELL

Have you noticed that in this message, up until this point, I had not even mentioned the one thing the average person thinks about relative to the torments of Hell? If you ask one hundred people what Hell is like, I suppose at least ninety-eight would reply that it is a lake of fire and brimstone. I deliberately did not mention this thus far in this message — except as it was in some verses which I quoted about some other matter — just to impress upon you the truth that this is the least of all the torments of Hell.

Do not misunderstand me, there is a *real* Hell of *real* fire which makes sinners grit their teeth in pain, cry out for water, and beg for mercy! Jude 7 says, "Even as Sodom and Gomorrha, and the cities about them in like manner, giving themselves over to fornication, and going after strange flesh, are set forth for an example, suffering the vengeance of eternal fire." Since it was *real* fire and *real* brimstone which destroyed Sodom and Gomorrha — and that was just a sample of Hell — we can expect *real* fire and *real* brimstone in the eternal land of the lost.

In all the Levitical sacrifices of the Old Testament showing God's hatred and punishment of sin there was *real* fire. The New Testament is just as emphatic! Without attempting to exhaust the Scripture on the subject, let me quote a few of the many references in the Bible which speak of eternal fire in Hell:

> But I say unto you, That whosoever is angry with his brother without a cause shall be in danger of the judgment: and whosoever shall say to his brother, Raca, shall be in danger of the council: but whosoever shall say, Thou fool, shall be in danger of hell fire (Matt. 5:22).

The Son of man shall send forth his angels, and they shall

gather out of his kingdom all things that offend, and them which do iniquity; And shall cast them into a furnace of fire: there shall be wailing and gnashing of teeth. . . . So shall it be at the end of the world: the angels shall come forth, and sever the wicked from among the just, And shall cast them into the furnace of fire: there shall be wailing and gnashing of teeth (Matt. 13: 41, 42, 49, 50).

Then shall he say also unto them on the left hand, Depart from me, ye cursed, into everlasting fire, prepared for the devil and his angels (Matt. 25:41).

And if thy hand offend thee cut it off: it is better for thee to enter into life maimed, than having two hands to go into hell, into the fire that never shall be quenched: Where their worm dieth not, and the fire is not quenched. And if thy foot offend thee, cut it off: it is better for thee to enter halt into life, than having two feet to be cast into hell, into the fire that never shall be quenched: Where their worm dieth not, and the fire is not quenched. And if thine eye offend thee, pluck it out: it is better for thee to enter into the kingdom of God with one eye, than having two eyes to be cast into hell fire: Where their worm dieth not, and the fire is not quenched. For every one shall be salted with fire, and every sacrifice shall be salted with salt (Mark 9:43-49).

The same shall drink of the wine of the wrath of God, which is poured out without mixture into the cup of his indignation; and he shall be tormented with fire and brimstone in the presence of the holy angels, and in the presence of the Lamb: And the smoke of their torment ascendeth up for ever and ever: and they have no rest day nor night, who worship the beast and his image, and whosoever receiveth the mark of his name (Rev. 14:10, 11).

And death and hell were cast into the lake of fire. This is the second death. And whosoever was not found written in the book of life was cast into the lake of fire (Rev. 20:14, 15).

But the fearful, and unbelieving, and the abominable, and murderers, and whoremongers, and sorcerers, and idolaters, and all liars, shall have their part in the lake which burneth with fire and brimstone: which is the second death (Rev. 21:8).

Fire produces the greatest possible physical pain known to mankind. The founder of Methodism, John Wesley, used to say: "Put your finger in the candle. Can you bear it for one minute? How then will you bear to have your body plunged into a lake of fire burning with brimstone?" This torment is indescribable!

Perhaps I had better sum up this message about the horrors of Hell by simply saying,

X. THE TORMENTS OF HELL ARE SO TERRIBLE GOD DOESN'T WANT ONE SINGLE SINNER TO GO THERE

How anxious God is to save sinners! It is not His desire for a single soul to enter into Hell and if you are eventually confined there for eternity it will be in opposition to the will of God for you. Ezekiel 33:11 says, "Say unto them, As I live, saith the Lord God, I have no pleasure in the death of the wicked; but that the wicked turn from his way and live: turn ye, turn ye from your evil ways; for why will ye die, O house of Israel?"

In answering the scoffer's criticism about the return of Christ, Peter said: "The Lord is not slack concerning his promise, as some men count slackness; but is longsuffering to us-ward, not willing that any should perish, but that all should come to repentance" (II Pet. 3:9). God does not desire that one single individual perish; He wants all to repent and be saved.

I Timothy 2:3, 4 expresses it: "For this is good and acceptable in the sight of God our Saviour; Who will have all men to be saved, and to come unto the knowledge of the truth." It is God's will that you be saved and come into the knowledge of His truth in Christ. If you go to Hell, it will be over the myriads of blockades God has placed on that broad road leading to destruction.

God does not want you in Hell, He wants you in Heaven! As a matter of fact, His desire for your salvation was so great He sent His only begotten Son all the way from the glories of Heaven to the horrors of Hell on the Cross just to buy your redemption and make it possible for you to be saved by faith in Him. John 5:24 quotes the Saviour as expressing it, "Verily, verily, I say unto you, He that heareth my word, and believeth on him that sent me, hath everlasting life, and shall not come into condemnation; but is passed from death unto life." If you will simply trust the Lord Christ, you will miss Hell and gain Heaven. However, it must be added that even God Himself cannot keep you out of Hell if you refuse to turn from your sin and accept the Lord Jesus Christ as your Saviour. Isaiah 33:14 contains a serious, solemn question for us to soberly consider:

"Who among us shall dwell with the devouring fire? who among us shall dwell with everlasting burnings?"

Think again of the awful torments of Hell! There is the terrible torment of association with the wicked, the awful torment of eternal separation from loved ones, both the redeemed and unredeemed, the terrifying torment of darkness, the agonizing torment of death in the form of separation from God and everything that comes from God, the agonizing torment of unspeakable sorrow, the torment of the scorpion sting of memory and the remorse of conscience, the torment of unsatisfied lustful cravings, the hopeless torment of despair, the burning torment of the unquenchable flame in brimstone and fire, and other torments so terrible God does not want a single soul damned in Hell.

Catherine Dangell expressed it,

> HELL! The prison house of despair.
> Here are some things that won't be there:
> No flowers will bloom on the banks of Hell,
> No beauties of nature we love so well;
> No comforts of home, music and song,
> No friendship of joy will be found in that throng;
> No children to brighten the long, weary night;
> No love nor peace nor one ray of light;
> No blood-washed soul with face beaming bright,
> No loving smile in the region of night;
> No mercy, no pity, no pardon nor grace,
> No water, oh, God, what a terrible place!
> The pangs of the lost no human can tell,
> Not one moment's ease — there is no rest in HELL!
>
> HELL! The prison house of despair.
> Here are some things that will be there:
> Fire and brimstone will be there, we know,
> For God in His Word has told us so;
> Memory, remorse, suffering and pain,
> Weeping and wailing, but all in vain;
> Blasphemers, swearers, haters of God,
> Christ-rejectors while here on earth trod;
> Murderers, gamblers, drunkards and liars,
> Will have their part in the lake of fire;
> The filthy, the vile, the cruel and mean,

What a horrible mob in Hell will be seen!
Yes, more than humans on earth can tell,
Are the torments and woes of eternal HELL!

Oh, thank God, dear reader, if you act now there *is* a way
out, there *is* a way of escape! You do not need to burn forever in the torments of Hell, you can be saved right now and
for all time. The Word of God says in John 1:11-13, "He came
unto his own, and his own received him not. But as many as
received him, to them gave he power to become the sons of
God, even to them that believe on his name: Which were born,
not of blood, nor of the will of the flesh, nor of the will of man,
but of God."

If you will now *receive* Christ Jesus as your personal Saviour
and *believe* in His Name, you will immediately become a child
of God with sins forever forgiven. In the light of the horrors
of this eternal Hell, will you not act right now and invite Him
into your heart? "Believe on the Lord Jesus Christ, and thou
shalt be saved, and thy house" (Acts 16:31).

Sinners, turn; why will ye die?
God, your Maker, asks you why:
God, who did your being give,
Made you with Himself to live:
He the fatal cause demands,
Asks the work of His own hands,
Why, ye thankless creatures, why
Will ye cross His love, and die?

Sinners, turn; why will ye die?
God, your Saviour, asks you why;
He, who did your souls retrieve,
Died Himself that ye might live.
Will ye let Him die in vain,
Crucify your Lord again?
Why, ye ransomed sinners, why
Will ye slight His grace, and die?

Sinners, turn; why will ye die?
God, the Spirit, asks you why;
God, who daily with you strove,
Wooed you to embrace His love.
Will ye not His grace receive?

Will ye still refuse to live?
Why, ye long-sought sinners, why
Will ye grieve your God, and die?

DECISION FOR CHRIST

Yes, sinner, *why will ye die?* Why should you spend an endless eternity in this Bible Hell when salvation has been provided freely for you by God Himself? We are plainly told about Jesus Christ in Acts 13:38, 39, "Be it known unto you therefore, men and brethren, that through this man is preached unto you the forgiveness of sins: And by him all that believe are justified from all things, from which ye could not be justified by the law of Moses."

Now is the time to settle your eternal destiny, making sure of entering Heaven, not Hell, the very instant you leave this life. If you will this moment put your faith and trust completely in the Lord Jesus Christ to save you from your sin, sign the form below as an outward indication of your inward decision. Then send a copy of the decision to me or write me a letter in your own words about what you have done. I will rejoice with you and send you a letter of encouragement and advice about the Christian life.

Evangelist Robert L. Sumner
P. O. Box 157
Brownsburg, Indiana 46112

Dear Brother Sumner:

I have read your Bible message, "Hell Is No Joke," and realize that I am a poor sinner who deserves to spend eternity in Hell because of my sin. However, I do not want to be lost. I want, instead, to take the Lord Jesus Christ as my personal Saviour and be sure of Heaven. *Right now, the best I know how, I do trust Him to forgive my sin, save me, and take me to Heaven.* I am honestly sorry for my past sin and failure and desire to do better. If the Lord will help me, I resolve to live according to His plan set forth in the Word of God. Please pray for me and send me some encouraging word of counsel about how to live a Christian life.

Signed _____

Address _____

_____

2

THE UNMOCKED GOD

> Be not deceived; God is not mocked: for whatsoever a man soweth, that shall he also reap.
>
> For he that soweth to his flesh shall of the flesh reap corruption; but he that soweth to the Spirit shall of the Spirit reap life everlasting (Gal. 6:7, 8).

"I want him out even if he kills me!"

So pleaded a Cleveland housewife, Mrs. Jane Kolodziej, while attempting to have her husband released from a psychiatric ward where he had been committed when she testified that he had threatened to kill her and their two sons. When she told the judge she believed her husband to be insane, the court had ordered him sent to the psychiatric ward.

Suddenly Mrs. Kolodziej decided that she wanted him back again, announced that she had lied to the court, and staged a four-day sit-down strike at the hospital. Finally she won his release by signing a waiver on which she made the statement, *"I want him out even if he kills me!"*

Three months later, husband Chester Kolodziej *beat her and the two children to death with a two-foot length of pipe.* She wanted her husband with her at any price, even life itself, and that is exactly the price she was compelled to pay.

When I read that story in a Los Angeles newspaper I thought of how so many millions of people, like this poor wife, want *sin* at any price, no matter what that price may be! Men sometimes think they want sin even though it will cost them sorrow, suffering and eternal heartbreak. They want sin although they *must* know it can be had only at the price of death, Hell and eternal damnation.

In this sermon and from this text I want to review again what you must pay as a price for your sin. You can *know* the price of sin according to the Word of the Living God and according to the testimony of multiplied human experience. These two, experience and revelation, are both unanimous and united in their definite, positive answer to this universal problem of mankind.

God has many laws which *cannot* be broken. Some of these unbreakable laws are in the natural realm. For example, there is the law which we call the law of gravity. If you step off the top of a fifty story building into space, you will surely and swiftly fall and be broken on the pavement below. You can *defy* that law, but you cannot *break* it!

Another example is the law we call the law of centrifugal force. If you drive your automobile around a sharp corner at the speed of one hundred miles an hour, your car will be unable to maintain its balance and will roll over a number of times. You can *defy* the law of centrifugal force, but you cannot *break* it.

Still another natural law of the Lord's pertains to the sowing and reaping of crops. If a farmer sows oats, the law of like-produces-like guarantees that the crop will be *oats*, never barley or wheat or something else. Whatever a farmer sows, he reaps!

But even as God has natural laws which cannot be broken, so He has strict spiritual laws impossible to defy without sorrow and suffering. The law of sowing and reaping, set forth in our text, is a tremendous example of His spiritual law. Remember, *it cannot be broken!* When God says something, that matter is fixed!

Examining these words, "Be not deceived; God is not mocked: for whatsoever a man soweth, that shall he also reap," the first thing that comes to my mind is

I. THE DESIRE OF THE DEVIL TO DELUDE

It is his business to try and deceive folks into believing they can mock God! He would have them think that they can sin and get by, that they can break holy laws and not get caught, that they can transgress without having to pay the price for their folly!

Come to think of it, how *successful* he has been in our generation! Young and old alike seem to have fallen for his subtle philosophy, "No one will ever know." They are like the little boy who, when asked by his Sunday school teacher which he had rather be of the two men in Christ's story of Luke 16 — the rich man or Lazarus — replied: "I'd rather be the rich man while I live, and Lazarus after I'm dead." They want to drink deeply from the fountains of this world's pleasures while on earth, then step into the glories of Heaven when they die. But it cannot be done; it is impossible to deceive or mock God for a single moment.

Numbers 32:23 says, "But if ye will not do so, behold, ye have sinned against the Lord: and be sure your sin will find you out." Like angry bloodhounds on the trail of a fleeing murderer, divine justice must overtake and punish your every transgression.

The psalmist, in the tenth Psalm, describes the apparent thoughts of the average sinner, when he writes: "He hath said in his heart, God hath forgotten: he hideth his face; he will never see it. . . . Wherefore doth the wicked contemn God? he hath said in his heart, Thou wilt not require it" (vv. 11, 13). But the very next verse continues, "Thou hast seen it; for thou beholdest mischief and spite, to requite it with thy hand . . ."

Proverbs 22:8 warns, "He that soweth iniquity shall reap vanity: and the rod of his anger shall fail." And Isaiah 3:11, after speaking of the blessing of the righteous, thunders forth: "Woe unto the wicked! it shall be ill with him: for the reward of his hands shall be given him." Yet some foolishly think they can mock God and get by with sin.

Wise, honest Abe Lincoln is reported to have said: "You can fool *all* of the people *some* of the time; you can fool *some* of the people *all* of the time; but you cannot fool *all* of the people *all* of the time!" To this sage bit of wisdom I would like to add the reminder: you cannot fool God *any* of the time!

I read one time of a man who, after committing a terrible deed, fled at night under cover of darkness, riding his horse furiously through the woods only to find at break of day he was back again at the scene of his crime, to be discovered, captured and condemned to die! The law of the spiritual harvest works somewhat like that. No matter how far or how fast the sinner may flee from his sin, somewhere, sometime, somehow, he will be faced with that sin again. It is inevitable! God cannot be mocked!

You cannot mock Him with a false profession. He knows who loves Him and who has just pretended to be saved. John 2:24, 25 records His reaction to a certain crowd who claimed to believe on Him: "But Jesus did not commit himself unto them, because he knew all men, And needed not that any should testify of man: for he knew what was in man."

You cannot mock Him with masses or confessionals to cover an ungodly life. Neither can you mock Him with supposed "good works" or sacrifices of time, money or talents. Just as a farmer could not mock nature by planting gravel dyed to look like wheat germs and receive a harvest of wheat, so it is impossible to mock God on matters of sin and salvation.

Not only does Satan try to deceive folks into thinking that they can mock God, but, failing here, he endeavors to fool them with his other lies. For example, a favorite deception of his is to convince sinners they must give up all their joys to become a Christian. *What a lie that is!* Actually, real joy doesn't start until one *is* a Christian! As the children sometimes sing:

> If you want joy, real joy, wonderful joy,
> Let Jesus come into your heart.

Dr. R. A. Torrey tells of dealing one time with a young girl who had swallowed this lie of the devil, feeling that there was too much to give up to become a Christian. The good doctor wisely asked her if she thought God loved her. Receiving a reply in the affirmative, he then asked *how much* God loved her.

She replied, "Enough to give His only Son for me upon the Cross of Calvary."

"Then," responded Dr. Torrey, "if He loves you that much, do you think He will insist upon your giving up anything that is good for you?"

"No!"

"Do you think you want to hold on to anything that is *not* for your good, that will do you harm?"

Hesitating a moment, she slowly replied, "No, I don't think I do."

"Then," persisted the faithful evangelist, "don't you think

you should take Christ as your personal Saviour *this very moment?*"

She acknowledged that she did, and in a matter of minutes was happy in the salvation of the Lord. That made good sense! And if you, like the prodigal son of hog-pen fame, will just "come to yourself," you will immediately claim Christ as your Saviour!

Another lie repeated quite successful by Satan through the centuries is that there is satisfaction in the pleasures of sin, but none in Christ. Actually, the very opposite is true. Satan has nothing that can satisfy for long. Like the "broken cisterns" of Israel's day, the fountains of sin "can hold no water" (Jer. 2:13). Only Jesus satisfies!

Satan baits his hook well with the love of money, enticing the sinner to look to riches in his quest for satisfaction. But those who have climbed to the summit on the mountain of wealth are almost unanimous in their voluminous confessions that it fails to satisfy.

Miss Rockefeller, daughter of the famous John D., is said to have replied to a reporter's question about her happiness, "No, I am not happy. And you may tell all and sundry who envy me that I am not happy at all."

The Mr. Eastman who headed the great Eastman Kodak film corporation stepped into a Rochester, New York, hotel room and put a bullet between his eyes. The Mr. Fleischmann of the yeast cake fame ended his life at Los Angeles, California, by plunging into the cold, dark waters of the blue Pacific. Jesse Livermore, one of Wall Street's greatest "bears," committed suicide. Ivar Krueger, who rose to be the head of one of the world's greatest monopolies, did the same. So did Leon Frazier, once president of the Bank of International Settlement. Dear friend, there is no peace, no satisfaction, no real joy in wealth.

The same is true of worldly pleasures and amusements. Satan seeks to convince all, especially young people, that there is more joy in the things of the world than in the things of God. Don't let him deceive you; it just isn't so! Countless thousands have believed his lie and ended up with blasted health, broken hearts and doomed souls!

Over a decade ago the pages of *The Sword of the Lord* told the pathetic story of a beautiful, twenty-two-year-old girl who died one winter at the Commercial Hospital in Cincinnati, Ohio.

She had come from a good home, had been well educated, talented and accomplished. However, sin was there and her fall took her into the vilest of vice and ruin. Dying in that hospital disgraced and brokenhearted, she left behind a poem of her own composition entitled, "The Beautiful Snow." This stirring poem is a masterpiece in its entirety, but let me give here just the last two verses which tell the truth of our text so vividly:

> Once I was fair as the beautfiul snow,
> With an eye like its crystals, a heart like its glow;
> Once I was loved for my innocent grace —
> Flattered and sought for the charm of my face,
> Father — Mother — Sisters — all:
> God and myself I have lost by my fall!
> The veriest wretch that goes shivering by
> Will keep a wide sweep lest I wander too nigh;
> For all that is on or about me, I know,
> There is nothing that's pure — but the beautiful snow.

> How strange it should be that this beautiful snow
> Should fall on a sinner with nowhere to go!
> How strange it would be, when the night comes again,
> If the snow and the ice struck my desperate brain;
> Fainting — Freezing — Dying alone —
> Too wicked for prayer, too weak for my moan
> To be heard in the crash of the crazy town
> Gone mad in the joy at the snow's coming down;—
> To lie and to die in my terrible woe,
> With a bed and a shroud of the beautiful snow!

Oh, the ruin, the wreck, the heartache of sin! Don't let the devil fool *you!* Don't be like this poor, wretched, fallen girl! Don't be deceived! God *cannot* be mocked!

But as I meditate upon this text I note another important Bible truth,

II. THE RULE THAT REGULATES THE REAPING

Our text declares, ". . . for *whatsoever* a man soweth, *that* shall he also reap." You are going to reap exactly what you sow; like begets like. This is what the Saviour said in Matthew 7:16 in His Sermon on the Mount. We read there, ". . . Do men gather grapes of thorns, or figs of thistles?" Obviously not! You must have a grapevine to gather grapes; you must have a fig tree to get figs! Never, *never* can you expect to gather grapes from a thorn bush or figs from thistle plants!

This observation of our text is also the lesson of experience. Eliphaz wisely reminded Job, "Even as I have seen, they that plow iniquity, and sow wickedness, reap the same. By the blast of God they perish, and by the breath of his nostrils are they consumed" (Job 4:8, 9). If you are going to sow to the flesh, then you must reap the corruption of the flesh. Some may reap *with* you, yes, but none can reap *for* you! You must harvest your own crop!

Jacob sadly discovered this truth in his life. Genesis 27 tells the shameful story of how he joined his mother Rebekah in deceiving Isaac into pronouncing upon him the blessing intended for Esau. Since, as Jacob said, "Esau my brother is a hairy man, and I am a smooth man" (v. 11), this called for some real strategy to fool the blinded Isaac. Verses 9 and 16 explain how they accomplished their crime: "Go now to the flock, and fetch me from thence two good kids of the goats; and I will make them savoury meat for thy father, such as he loveth. . . . And she put the skins of the kids of the goats upon his hands, and upon the smooth of his neck." Then, when blind Isaac felt of his hands and found them hairy, he pronounced the blessing, thinking it was the elder son, Esau.

After Jacob's sin in deception *by the kid of the goats* had gained him the blessing, he fled the country from the wrathful Esau, feeling, no doubt, that he had succeeded in his sin. But *had* he?

Later in Jacob's life he was the happy father of twelve sons, one of whom, Joseph, was a special delight in his old age. But tragedy struck that household and his ten elder sons came home from tending their flocks one day to show him his favorite's "coat of many colours" covered with blood. Immediately he surmised that Joseph had been devoured by "an evil beast" and was "without doubt rent in pieces" (Gen. 37:33). Actually, the older sons were deceiving him, for they had spitefully sold Joseph, through envy, to slavery in Egypt, where later God placed him in supreme power.

How were they able to deceive Jacob? The record, in Genesis 37:31, says, "And they took Joseph's coat, and killed a kid of the goats, and dipped the coat in the blood." That's right! Jacob was deceived even as he had deceived, *by the kid of the goats!* Jacob was merely reaping the bitter crop of the wicked seed he had sown some thirty years before. His sin had found him out; his own chickens had come home to roost!

What Jacob sadly discovered about the law of sowing and reaping applies to all. Men reap exactly what they sow. If you sow a life without God and His Christ, you are certain to reap an eternity without God and His Christ!

If a farmer kept sowing his fields with seed every year but just as surely never reaped a crop, he would be considered a fool. Yet the average man feels he can sow his seeds of sin — "wild oats" he calls them — and never reap a bitter crop when the "oats" come to harvest. No wonder God calls that man a fool!

What kind of fool would a man be if he sowed his entire six hundred acre farm with thistle seed, expecting to reap corn, wheat or barley? Then what about the man who sows his whole life with the seeds of sin, yet expects to enter God's glorious Heaven the moment he dies? "Whatsoever a man soweth, *that* shall he also reap"! This principle works in family life, in business life, in social life, in church life, and in all other fields as well.

One summer I spent quite a bit of time at the home of my brother-in-law in a small Illinois coal mining community. I remember sitting on the front porch in the cool of the day many, many times and watching little boys and little girls coming back from the saloons uptown with dinner buckets full of beer for the lazy miner daddies at home. Oh, would God that He could lift a curtain from before the eyes of those fathers to let them see into the future. Perhaps they would witness a prison cell and a sunken-eyed, dejected, defeated, vile-of-lip, bestial criminal in death row. Horrified, they might cry out, "My God, who is he?" only to hear the answer from the skies, "That is the boy you sent for your evening beer back in Illinois. Remember?" Yes, you will reap whatsoever you sow!

Of course, *good* sowing will bring *good* reaping. Our text brings that out with the words: ". . . but he that soweth to the Spirit shall of the Spirit reap life everlasting." Ecclesiastes 11:1 says, "Cast thy bread upon the waters: for thou shalt find it after many days." And Galatians 6:9, 10 adds, "And let us not be weary in well doing: for in due season we shall reap, if we faint not. As we have therefore opportunity, let us do good unto all men, especially unto them who are of the household of faith."

Sowing which includes soul-winning, kindness, helpfulness, offerings, sacrifices, and other forms of Christian service will bring a bountiful harvest of blessed reaping and reward. It pays to *live* right; it pays to *do* right!

Men, women and young people who live for Christ reap big dividends during their earthly lives; they will reap big dividends in eternity. Proverbs 11:18 says, "The wicked worketh a deceitful work: but to him that soweth righteousness shall be a sure reward." And Isaiah 3:10 promises, "Say ye to the righteous, that it shall be well with him: for they shall eat the fruit of their doings"!

On the other hand, evil sowing will bring certain evil reaping. Some people consistently refuse to realize this, but it is nonetheless true. The same folks who deny it in their actions would call you a raving maniac if you suggested to them sowing wheat, hoping for a harvest of corn!

Often you hear people foolishly remark, "Oh, well, all young people have to sow their wild oats!" I don't know when the devil first started this vicious lie — it was popular long before my time — but I do know that young folks (and old folks, too) who *sow* wild oats must *reap* wild oats. In the words of Eliphaz again, "Even as I have seen, they . . . reap the same" (Job 4:8). Yes, the folly of youth sometimes forgets the certain harvest, *here* and *hereafter!*

But there is still a third thought that should be mentioned relative to the law of the harvest and that is the truth concerning

III. THE SURPLUS THAT SUCCEEDS THE SOWING

Dear sinner, you will not only reap just what you sow, you will reap much, much more than you sow! This is simply the law of sowing and reaping. The farmer who sows one hundred bushels of wheat plans to reap many, many times that amount when harvest time comes. *It is the same with sin!* Hosea 8:7 declared of idolatrous Samaria, "For they have sown the wind, and they shall reap the whirlwind. . . ." Sinners who sow the wind in sin must expect to reap a whirlwind in judgment!

Sometimes farmers have crop failures due to droughts, bugs, pestilences, hail, excessive rain and various other causes, but with the sowing of sin comes no harvest failures. The apostle stresses this truth in Romans 2:6-11 when he declares that God

> . . . will render to every man according to his deeds: To them who by patient continuance in well doing seek for glory and honour and immortality, eternal life: But unto them that are contentious, and do not obey the truth, but obey unrighteousness, indignation and wrath, Tribulation and anguish, upon every soul of man that doeth evil, of the Jew first, and also of the Gentile; But glory, honour, and peace, to every man that worketh good, to the Jew first, and also to the Gentile: For there is no respect of persons with God.

David, a man who rose high yet sank low through sin, sadly learned this truth following his planting the seeds of lust's most terrible twin transgressions: adultery and murder! King David sowed to the wind and reaped the whirlwind; his sins paid off four-to-one!

The first crop he harvested from that ill-fated sowing was the death of his beautiful, dearly beloved baby boy. Who could adequately describe the heart anguish of that man witnessing the cold corpse of his flesh and blood lowered into the ground — and all the time knowing *it was his sin* finding him out that had caused it?

The second harvest was reaped when his son Amnon, overwrought with the vilest of passions, deceived and then forcibly ruined by rape his half-sister, David's daughter Tamar, stealing forever her most noble possession of virtue. Understandably, this crop was more bitter for David to harvest than the first.

The third season of reaping arrived when David's son Absalom ignored the Biblical command to leave vengeance in the Lord's hands and slew Amnon at a banquet planned for the occasion.

But the fourth harvest of the single sowing was perhaps the hardest of all for David to bear. Absalom, forgiven by David for the murder of Amnon, came home only to steal the love of the people from his father and drive David from the throne. In the resulting battle, against specific orders by the king himself,

Absalom was slain by David's men. The anguish and grief brought to the soul of David at this harvest is described in the last verse of II Samuel 18 and the first verse of chapter 19: "And the king was much moved, And went up to the chamber over the gate, and wept: and as he went, thus he said, O my son Absalom, my son, my son Absalom! would God I had died for thee, O Absalom, my son, my son! And it was told Joab, Behold, the king weepeth and mourneth for Absalom."

Yes, David's sin had found him out; his chickens had come home to roost!

There will be a surplus *in this life* for those who sow the seeds of sin. You will reap the harvest in your body, in your character, in your conscience, in your children and in a multitudinous host of other ways. Simply because your sin does not find you out immediately, do not feel that you have escaped the inevitable law of the harvest! Some harvests ripen immediately, as was the case for the woman of John 8 who was caught in the very act of sin, but usually there is a long delay between seedtime and reaping.

Ecclesiastes 8:11-13 warns: "Because sentence against an evil work is not executed speedily, therefore the heart of the sons of men is fully set in them to do evil. Though a sinner do evil an hundred times, and his days be prolonged, yet surely I know that it shall be well with them that fear God, which fear before Him: But it shall not be well with the wicked, neither shall he prolong his days, which are as a shadow; because he feareth not before God."

Do not think that because sentence is not "executed speedily" that you have gotten by with your sin. Remember, "The mills of God grind slowly, but they grind exceedingly small."

Recall also how long the harvest was delayed in the life of wicked Queen Jezebel! She, through trickery, lying and murder, stole Naboth's vineyard for equally wicked King Ahab. Elijah met them as they viewed the stolen possession, pronouncing a curse upon Ahab, saying, ". . . Thus saith the Lord, In the place where dogs licked the blood of Naboth shall dogs lick thy blood, even thine," and upon Jezebel with the words, "And of Jezebel also spake the Lord, saying, The dogs shall eat Jezebel by the wall of Jezreel" (I Kings 21:19, 23).

Three years later the prophecy concerning Ahab was fulfilled to the very letter, but Jezebel continued unmolested for nearly a score of years. Was she to get by with her sin; had she outsmarted the law of the harvest? II Kings 9 describes how Jehu came to Jezreel where Jezebel was staying, had her thrown from the palace window to the stones below where he rode his horses and chariot over her prostrate, bloodied form. Going into the palace to eat and drink, he suddenly relented and ordered the servants to give her a decent burial "for she is a king's daughter." But when they went to dispose of her remains, "they found no more of her than the skull, and the feet, and the palms of her hands" (v. 35). The dogs had eaten her flesh by the wall of Jezreel *just as the Lord had spoken;* Jezebel's chickens had come home to roost, her sin had finally found her out.

I think also of how long Satan has escaped Hell, how long he has apparently been getting by with his sin. For over six thousand years now — how much longer only God knows — Satan has been rebelling against the Will and the Word of Almighty God, still free to manifest his wickedness. But Revelation 20:10 foretells the day when justice will find him out, "And the devil that deceived them was cast into the lake of fire and brimstone . . . and shall be tormented day and night for ever and ever."

Over a hundred years ago archeologists found a well-preserved mummy in an Egyptian tomb. Hieroglyphic experts agreed that the writing on the mummy cloth dated back to the early Pharaohs and that the burial date was about that time. When they took the mummy to the British Museum they examined it more closely, finding seeds in its hand. Curiously, they took those several thousand year old seeds and planted them, expecting nothing to come of it. But in due time a vine sprang from the soil which was a proper specimen of what any vine should be! Life had been wrapped up in those seeds for centuries, sprouting forth when given the right opportunity.

Sin is like those seeds! Never forget that God has *your* seeds, and one day they'll sprout again! ". . . Be sure your sin will find you out"!

But not only will you reap the harvest of your iniquity in this life, you are also going to reap it *in the life to come.*

Hebrews 9:27 solemnly declares, ". . . it is appointed unto men once to die, but after this the judgment."

Revelation 20:11-15 describes it:

> And I saw a great white throne, and him that sat on it, from whose face the earth and the heaven fled away; and there was found no place for them. And I saw the dead, small and great, stand before God; and the books were opened: and another book was opened, which is the book of life: and the dead were judged out of those things which were written in the books, according to their works. And the sea gave up the dead which were in it: and death and hell delivered up the dead which were in them; and they were judged every man according to their works. And death and hell were cast into the lake of fire. This is the second death. And whosoever was not found written in the book of life was cast into the lake of fire.

Dear friend, God *cannot* be mocked! One day you will face Him to give an account for *your* sins! What will you say? What excuse will you offer for your sin and for your rejection of Christ? Why not trust Christ as your personal Saviour right now and escape that judgment? Romans 10:13 guarantees, "For whosoever shall call upon the name of the Lord shall be saved!" Will you call?

> Sowing the seed by the daylight fair,
> Sowing the seed by the noonday glare,
> Sowing the seed by the fading light,
> Sowing the seed in the solemn night;
> Oh, what shall the harvest be?
> Oh, what shall the harvest be?
>
> Sowing the seed by the wayside high,
> Sowing the seed on the rocks to die,
> Sowing the seed where the thorns will spoil,
> Sowing the seed in the fertile soil;
> Oh, what shall the harvest be?
> Oh, what shall the harvest be?
>
> Sowing the seed of a ling'ring pain,
> Sowing the seed of a madden'd brain,
> Sowing the seed of a tarnished name,
> Sowing the seed of eternal shame;
> Oh, what shall the harvest be?
> Oh, what shall the harvest be?

Sowing the seed of an aching heart,
Sowing the seed while the tear-drops start,
Sowing in hope till the reapers come,
Gladly to gather the harvest home;
Oh, what shall the harvest be?
Oh, what shall the harvest be?

"Be not deceived; God is not mocked: for whatsoever a man soweth, that shall he also reap. For he that soweth to his flesh shall of the flesh reap corruption; but he that soweth to the Spirit shall of the Spirit reap life everlasting."

O SINNER, WHY TRY TO MOCK GOD? WHY TRY TO GET BY WITH SIN?

You have read this sermon with its strong, Scriptural warning. Surely your heart must have been convicted. Do you think you can sin and get by? Do you think you can continue to insult God and escape eternal destruction? Now let me earnestly invite you to seek peace with God today, to run to Him for mercy.

Jesus Christ died for our sins. By His sacrifice on the Cross, He paid the debt of every poor sinner. The only hope, the only way of escape, the only possible salvation for any mortal is to repent of sin and trust Jesus Christ for forgiveness and salvation. Will you do that today? The blessed promise of John 3:16 is, "For God so loved the world, that he gave his only begotten Son, that whosoever believeth in him should not perish, but have everlasting life." God loves you. Jesus died for you. If you will this moment honestly turn your heart from sin, will rely upon Jesus Christ for forgiveness, will surrender to Him, accept Him, trust Him as your own Saviour, He will forgive your sins this moment. He waits to change your heart, make you a child of God and assure you of a home in Heaven. Will you trust Him now? Will you make the grand and eternal choice between sin and the Saviour?

In the sermon, I quoted the sad poem written by the dying girl in Cincinnati who had bitterly discovered the tragic pay-off of sin. After her death a servant of the Lord added another verse to the poem which presents the other side of the truth;

Helpless and foul as the trampled snow,
Sinner, despair not! Christ stoopeth low
To rescue the soul that is lost in sin,
And raise it to life and enjoyment again.
Groaning — Bleeding — Dying for thee,
The Crucified hung on th' accursed tree!
His accents of mercy fall soft on thine ear:
"There is mercy for thee,"— He will hear thy weak prayer.
"O God, in the stream that for sinners did flow,
Wash me, and I shall be whiter than snow."

Oh, decide today! Then please sign the form below as a solemn expression of your faith and copy it in a letter and mail it to me today. I will rejoice with you and will write you a letter of counsel and encouragement. Decide, sign the statement, and mail me the glad news of your decision today!

Evangelist Robert L. Sumner
P. O. Box 157
Brownsburg, Indiana 46112

Dear Brother Sumner:

I have read your gospel sermon, "The Unmocked God." I believe what the Bible says, that one cannot get by with sin, that Christ is the only Saviour, that He stands ready to pardon and save those who trust in Him. This moment I turn to Jesus Christ and accept Him as my own personal Saviour. Here and now I renounce sin in my heart. I confess myself to be a poor, lost sinner and I depend upon Jesus Christ this moment to save me. By His help I set out to live for Him and will claim Him openly as my Saviour.

Signed ....

Address ....

....

3

SLIPPING INTO HELL

Therefore we ought to give the more earnest heed to the things which we have heard, lest at any time we should let them slip.

For if the word spoken by angels was stedfast, and every transgression and disobedience received a just recompence of reward;

How shall we escape, if we neglect so great salvation; which at the first began to be spoken by the Lord, and was confirmed unto us by them that heard him;

God also bearing them witness, both with signs and wonders, and with divers miracles, and gifts of the Holy Ghost, according to his own will? (Heb. 2:1-4).

Years ago a mighty ocean steamer was silently ploughing its way across the majestic Atlantic when the spine-chilling scream pierced the air, "Man overboard!" In the immediate excitement and confusion that followed the first tragic announcement, one well-dressed businessman raced across the deck crying, "That man is my brother! I'll pay $5,000 to the one who saves him!"

Seemingly in no time at all a lifeboat had been lowered and, as passengers and crew alike lined the rail shouting cheers of encouragement, the drowning man was pulled into the lifeboat and returned to the steamer. A strong rope was lowered from the ship to the lifeboat, steady hands fastened it under the arms of the victim, and the signal to hoist away was given. Higher and higher they lifted him until finally, just as they were about to pull him over the rail of the vessel to safety, the rope slipped and the man fell, hitting the prow of the lifeboat, then sank into the Atlantic without ever surfacing again.

This true incident is a modern parable representing myriads of men and women in our twentieth century. Unnumbered thousands have been brought to the very threshold of salvation, have acknowledged that they were lost sinners on the road to Hell, have admitted that the finished work of Christ could fully save them, have literally trembled with the pungent conviction of the Holy Spirit's persistent pleading to trust Christ; but have steadfastly refused to make their decision and eventually slipped away into Hell.

It was not that they consciously hated Christ — they merely neglected His so great salvation. It was not that they did not believe the Bible — they just put off settling things with God. It was not that they preferred Hell to Heaven — they just never got around to saying "Yes" to the Saviour. It was not that they bitterly rejected Christ — they only blithely neglected Him. They simply slipped into Hell, blindly drifting to eternal death, doom and damnation.

Ponder well these words of God in our text. They soberly warn us of the solemn seriousness of sin and salvation. They form a tremendous "yea" and "amen" to the tragic truth of Proverbs 29:1, "He, that being often reproved hardeneth his neck, shall suddenly be destroyed, and that without remedy." They comprise a reaffirmation of the Saviour's statements in Mark 8:36, 37, "For what shall it profit a man, if he shall gain the whole world, and lose his own soul? Or what shall a man give in exchange for his soul?"

The salvation and security of your soul is still the most important thing of time or eternity. As the poet has penned:

> To lose your wealth is much,
> To lose your health is more,
> To lose your soul is such a loss
> As no man can restore.

Yet many more people die unsaved and wind up in Hell than trust Christ as their Saviour and reach Heaven. The authority for this startling statement is none other than the decider of the destinies of men, the Lord Jesus Christ. He plainly taught this truth when He said, "Enter ye in at the strait gate: for wide is the gate, and broad is the way, that leadeth to destruction, and many there be which go in thereat: Because strait is the gate, and narrow is the way, which leadeth unto life, and few there be that find it" (Matt. 7:13, 14).

Why is this true? With all the passionate conviction of my soul punctuating every syllable, I reply that our text is the answer for the majority: *they neglect so great salvation!* It is not that they disbelieve the Bible, not that they do not want to be saved, not that they do not intend to be saved some day, but that they *put off* their decision until finally it is "too late" and Hell is their portion forever.

"Give the more earnest heed" (v. 1) as I call again to your attention some of the vital truths God has set forth in this text. Consider with me first,

I. THE PUNISHMENT OF SIN

The second verse reminds us that "the word spoken by angels was stedfast, and every transgression and disobedience received a just recompense of reward." Sin *must* be punished! *Every* sin must be punished! God would no longer be God if He let sin go by unnoticed, unjudged and unpunished. Such an unthinkable thing would be a defeat for Him, a triumph for Satan. But the devil is *not* going to win in this matter and sin *is* going to be punished.

A. *All Sin Must Come to Judgment*

Ecclesiastes 12:14 affirms it with the words, "For God shall bring every work into judgment, with every secret thing, whether it be good, or whether it be evil." In the eleventh chapter of the same book, verse 9, Solomon said, "Rejoice, O young man, in thy youth; and let thy heart cheer thee in the days of thy youth, and walk in the ways of thine heart, and in the sight of thine eyes; but know thou, that for all these things God will bring thee into judgment."

The Lord Jesus Christ defined it still closer when He declared in Matthew 12:36, "But I say unto you, That every idle word that men shall speak, they shall give account thereof in the day of judgment."

Oh, listen to what God has repeatedly vowed: Every sin that you commit, whether large or small, must be brought into judgment, and it must be punished. You are not going to put anything over on Him! Those secret sins you *thought* you got away with will be brought to light at the judgment bar of God. As the consecrated hymn writer expressed it:

Every secret lust and tho't,
There shall be to judgment bro't
When the Lord in all His glory shall appear;
All the deeds of darkest night
Shall come out to greet the light
When I stand before the judgment bar.

B. *Punished Justly According to Works*

But not only will every sin be punished, it will be punished *justly!* "Every transgression and disobedience received a *just* recompense of reward," says our text. The corroborating testimony of Psalm 9:7, 8 insists, "But the Lord shall endure for ever: he hath prepared his throne for judgment. And he shall judge the world *in righteousness,* he shall minister judgment to the people *in uprightness.*" Then Acts 17:31 confirms this truth with the words, "Because he hath appointed a day, in the which he will judge the world *in righteousness* by that man whom he hath ordained; whereof he hath given assurance unto all men, in that he hath raised him from the dead." And the positive note of Romans 2:2 declares, "But we are *sure* that the judgment of God *is according to truth. . . .*"

You will be judged fairly, justly, in righteousness, in uprightness and according to truth. All men will be judged "according to their works," as we are told twice in the twentieth chapter of Revelation which deals with the Great Judgment Morning. The scales of justice will then truly balance for the first time since Eve partook of the forbidden fruit in the historic Garden of Eden.

C. *Murder, Adultery, Cursing, Lying, Not Greatest Sins*

Since sin will be punished justly, the greatest sin will demand the greatest punishment, of course. *But what is the greatest sin?* If you were to ask one hundred men that question, you might get one hundred entirely different answers.

One would say, "The greatest sin is murder!" Murder *is* a terrible, tragic, unholy sin. One of the Ten Commandments warns against it, saying, "Thou shalt not kill" (Ex. 20:13). This sin is one so vile it demands the supreme penalty of death inflicted upon those who are guilty. Genesis 9:6 insists, "Whoso sheddeth man's blood, by man shall his blood be shed: for in the image of God made he man." America could quench a great majority of her thirty-six murders a day — one every forty minutes — if she would get back to the law of God and put every murderer at the end of a rope, in an electric chair, or in a gas chamber. But as horrible a sin as is murder, this is not the greatest.

Someone else strongly exclaims, "Adultery is the greatest sin!" Here, too, is a hideous offense against both God and man, greater even, in my estimation, than murder. God hates adultery so vehemently that He allows it as a possible grounds for divorce — absolutely the only sin for which He permits the breaking of the holy marriage bonds. Furthermore, adultery is such a heinous sin that God originally demanded the death penalty for it. Exodus 20:14 declared, "Thou shalt not commit adultery," and Leviticus 20:10 added, ". . . the man that committeth adultery with another man's wife, even he that committeth adultery with his neighbor's wife, the adulterer and the adulteress shall surely be put to death." In Proverbs 6:32 God declared, "But whoso committeth adultery with a woman lacketh understanding: he that doeth it destroyeth his own soul." But even adultery is not the greatest sin!

Another speaks out, saying, "I think cursing is the greatest sin." Cursing is a great sin! God said in Exodus 20:7, another of the Ten Commandments, "Thou shalt not take the name of the Lord thy God in vain; for the Lord will not hold him guiltless that taketh his name in vain." He also said, in Leviticus 24:16, "He that blasphemeth the name of the Lord, he shall surely be put to death, and all the congregation shall certainly stone him: as well the stranger, as he that is born in the land, when he blasphemeth the name of the Lord, shall be put to death."

Cursing is a cheap, lowly sin showing the depravity of the heart and the emptiness of the head. It is a dual sign of ignorance and corruption. Show me a man or a woman who curses and I will show you an empty-headed individual with a dirty, rotten, black, sinful heart. It is a sin once confined to pool halls, saloons, brothels, and the like, but now is apt to be heard anywhere — from the White House down.

William R. Newell tells of one time seeing the world's heavyweight boxing champion. A man near him said, "Boy, I'd sure hate to be hit by that man." He had fear for another man.

But just a moment later the same man was profanely taking the Name of the Lord in vain. There was "no fear of God before [his] eyes" (Rom. 3:18). Exodus 20:7 meant nothing to him then, but it will when he stands before Him who said, "I will not hold him guiltless that taketh my name in vain." But even cursing is not the greatest sin!

Someone else questions, "Is it lying?" Here again we have another truly terrible transgression. In verse 8 and 27 of Revelation 21, God classes lying with murder, drunkenness, idolatry, adultery, sorcery and such sins. I have no respect at all for a liar and of all the multitudinous sins of mankind I have more difficulty being charitable and forgiving with reference to it than any other. But there is a sin far greater than lying!

Neither is covetousness, stealing, slander, gossip, booze-guzzling, wife-beating, sodomy, witchcraft, hypocrisy or unthankfulness the greatest sin! Fortunately, God has not left us to our own imaginations as to what is the gravest sin deserving the greatest punishment.

D. Christ-Rejection the Greatest Sin

On the highest authority of the universe, I declare unto you that the greatest sin in all the world is the sin of unbelief, of rejecting Jesus Christ as your personal Saviour, of not giving your whole heart to God!

In Mark 12:29, 30, responding to the scribe's question, "Which is the first commandment of all?" the Lord Jesus declared, "The first of all the commandments is, Hear, O Israel; The Lord our God is one Lord: And thou shalt love the Lord thy God with all thy heart, and with all thy soul, and with all thy mind, and with all thy strength: this is the first commandment." Since this is the first and greatest commandment, to break it is the sin first in importance and greatest in scope. It is not the harlot who has committed the greatest sin; it is the woman who does not love God. It is not the drunkard, not the murderer, not the criminal; it is the man who has not given his heart to God; *it is the Christ-rejector.*

The Saviour said the same thing in John 16:9 while explaining the Holy Spirit's ministry in reproving the lost of sin: "Of sin, because they believe not on me." This is the only sin, if continued, God cannot forgive. It is a sin so awful, so terrible, so hideous, so heinous that it deserves all the righteous wrath of a holy God poured out upon the sinner without measure forever! This is an eternal sin against the Eternal Christ demanding an eternal penalty.

Surely you will admit that it is right and proper for the greatest sin to receive the greatest punishment! Therefore the only sin of which you need be guilty to damn your soul in the fire and brimstone of Hell for an eternity is this one of not giving your heart to God, the sin of rejecting Jesus Christ as Saviour.

But it is so needless for a sinner to perish! Would it be foolish to drown with a life preserver within grasp? Would it be senseless to burn to death in a fiery building if a ladder awaiting your use reached from your window to the ground? Would it be ridiculous for a man who had accidently swallowed poison to reject the antidote when placed to his lips by a friendly hand? Would it be folly for the pilot of a crashing jet to refuse to press the ejection button at his fingertip which would throw him free to safety and life? In like manner, it is exceedingly foolish for a sinner to die in his sins and pay the penalty himself for his own transgressions when full, free salvation could be his for the asking.

Black indeed is the picture of the punishment of sin, but God has not left us without remedy. He, in His mercy and love, has provided a "so great salvation." Note with me next,

II. THE PROVISION OF SALVATION

The third verse of our text questions, "How shall we escape, if we neglect so great salvation?" The "so great" of this passage is as completely beyond description or understanding as the "so loved" of John 3:16 where we are told, "God so loved the world, that he gave his only begotten Son."

A. *Great Origin of "So Great Salvation"*

This salvation is *so great* because of its *Creator!* It was conceived, not in the halls of Congress, not on the floors of conventions, not in the rooms of Parliament, but in the very glory-circled throne room of Heaven! Confucianism, Buddhism, Shintoism, Hinduism, Mohammedanism, Modernism and all other false ideologies were planned in the pit of Tophet by the master deceiver himself, but this in the palace of the Trinity with God the Father, God the Son, and God the Holy Spirit as co-equal Counselors! It was not conceived by mortal men, but by the immortal, eternal, unchanging Lord of Heaven and earth. It is but the outgrowth of the love of the holy, all-powerful God for your poor, sinful, lost, Hell-bent, Hell-bound soul. This salvation is so great because of its Creator.

B. *Tremendous Cost Makes This a Great Salvation*

Again, it is *so great* because of its *cost.* In I Peter 1:18, 19 we read, "Forasmuch as ye know that ye were not redeemed with corruptible things, as silver and gold, . . . But with the precious blood of Christ, as of a Lamb without blemish and without spot." Take the debts of all the wars of all the people from the beginning of creation, add them together, then multiply them by the total number of stars in the firmament. Turn that fantastically unbelievable figure into thousand dollar bills and you would not have enough money to even begin paying the price of salvation.

The price it takes to purchase redemption is the supreme price of the ages: the highest, the greatest that God Himself could offer. It took the gift of the Father's only begotten Son! It took the Saviour's gift of His living, loving, sinless self at Calvary to blot out your sins and purchase redemption for you! The cost was so tremendous that the sun hid its face and refused to look; the earth trembled and shook with fear beneath the load when the Son of God "paid the price" with His own precious blood for man's salvation. It is so great because of its cost.

C. *Grandly Complete Salvation*

Again, it is *so great* because of its *completeness!* Colossians 2:9, 10 tells us, "For in him [Christ] dwelleth all the fulness of the Godhead bodily. And ye are complete in him . . ." There is absolutely nothing truly great, nothing spiritually great, nothing eternally great that is not included for the child of God in Jesus Christ our Lord. We receive the forgiveness of all our sins, a new heart, a new nature, the indwelling Holy Spirit of God, joy, peace, assurance, the privilege of prayer to a Father who delights in answering, sanctification, power for victory over sin and Satan, and a host of other innumerable benefits in this life. *All this, and then Heaven, too!*

Ephesians 1:3 describes it, "Blessed be the God and Father of our Lord Jesus Christ, who hath blessed us with all spiritual blessings in heavenly places in Christ." Peter encourages those who "have obtained like precious faith . . . through the righteousness of God and our Saviour Jesus Christ" with the words, "Grace and peace be multiplied unto you through the knowledge of God, and of Jesus our Lord, According as his divine power hath given unto us all things that pertain unto life and godliness, through the knowledge of him that hath called us to glory and virtue: Whereby are given unto us exceeding great and precious promises . . ." (II Pet. 1:2-4). And Romans 8:32 adds, "He that spared not his own Son, but delivered him up for us all, how shall he not with him also freely give us all things?"

This so great salvation is complete because of what we have included with its scope, but also because "It is finished" (John 19:30). Jesus paid it *all!* There is nothing left for us to do to earn it, buy it, merit it, or finish it. It is ours complete just for the taking.

The biographers of Hudson Taylor tell how, when he was just a lad of fifteen, the words, "The finished work of Christ," in a booklet he was reading suddenly arrested his attention. He began musing about why the writer used those words until suddenly the thought struck him with amazing clarity, "If the whole work is finished, the whole debt paid, what is there left for me to do?"

In a moment the answer dawned upon the heart of the boy who was to become the founder of the China Inland Mission, so that he later said, "There was nothing in the world for me to do save to fall upon my knees, and accepting this Saviour and His salvation to praise Him for evermore." Yes, this so great salvation is fully complete, simply awaiting the acceptance of the sinner.

D. *So Great Salvation for All the World*

Again, this salvation is *so great* because of its *circumference.* It reaches North and South America, Europe, Asia, Africa, and the islands of the sea. It goes to the north and the south, the east and the west, wherever man is found. The hymn writer exclaimed,

> It goes beyond the highest star,
> And reaches to the lowest hell!

The rich and the poor, the harlots and the queens, the drunkards and the presidents, the Catholics and the Protestants, the Jews and the Gentiles, the bound and the free, the black and the white, the ignorant and the lettered, are all included. God's salvation is for folks on either side of the tracks who will accept it freely. The poet has well said,

> None are excluded thence
> But they who do themselves exclude.

Jesus Christ, who cannot lie, has guaranteed, ". . . him that cometh to me I will in no wise cast out" (John 6:37). The God who swears by Himself "because he could swear by no greater" (Heb. 6:13) has sworn, "For whosoever shall call upon the name of the Lord shall be saved" (Rom. 10:13). And the closing invitation in the Bible promises, ". . . let him that is athirst come. And whosoever will, let him take the water of life freely" (Rev. 22:17). Anyone who wants to can get in on this so great salvation.

E. *Salvation So Great Because Free Gift to Believers*

Not only is this salvation *so great* because of its Creator, because of its cost, because of its completeness, and because of its circumference, but also because of its *conditions*.

What are the conditions for receiving this salvation? One is that it be received *freely!* There must be no price of any kind paid by the receiver. It is a gift; there is to be nothing down and nothing to pay. Ephesians 2:8, 9 describes it with the words, "For by grace are ye saved through faith; and that not of yourselves: it is the gift of God: Not of works, lest any man should boast." The Saviour's salvation is what Isaiah 55:1 refers to as being "without money and without price!" Oh, reader, believe it: *it's free!*

The other condition attached to this so great salvation is *faith!* The only Biblical answer to the question, "Sirs, what must I do to be saved?" is simply, "Believe on the Lord Jesus Christ, and thou shalt be saved" (Acts 16:30, 31). Any other answer is not a Bible answer. You need only take it, accept it, receive it!

John 1:12 says, "As many as received him, to them gave he power to become the sons of God, even to them that believe on his name." And John 3:16, familiar and loved by millions, assures us, "For God so loved the world, that he gave his only begotten Son, that whosoever believeth in him should not perish, but have everlasting life."

Oh, do not make it difficult when it is so simple! This eternal salvation is yours forever the very moment you receive Jesus Christ as your personal Saviour. Delay accepting Him no longer.

> Just now, your doubtings give o'er;
> Just now, reject Him no more;
> Just now, throw open the door;
> Let Jesus come into your heart.

But since the punishment for sin is so tremendously awful and the provision of salvation so wonderfully glorious, the third great truth of our text is exceedingly difficult to realize; that is,

III. THE PROCRASTINATION OF SINNERS

What amazement the angels of Heaven and the demons of Hell alike must register in viewing sinking, Hell-bound sinners procrastinating, putting off, neglecting to accept this so great salvation freely offered them in Christ. Verse 3 of our text asks, "How shall we escape, if we neglect so great salvation?"

Billy Sunday insisted that this question is unanswerable. Preaching to a great crowd in a union revival meeting at Omaha, Nebraska, more than forty years ago, he said:

> If I should go to your leading merchant, and he would describe to me the principles necessary to pursue in order to carry a business to a successful issue, I would thank him for the information, then ask him the question of my text, and I would turn without an answer.
>
> Should I go to your leading physician or physicians and they would explain to me many things about materia medica and medical jurisprudence, and then I would ask them the question of my text, I would turn and leave them without an answer.
>
> Should I go to the lost world and if I should stand before the bars of their eternal imprisonment in Hell and look at their

faces as they leered at me, and read upon their foreheads, "No hope"; if I should ask them the question of my text, I would turn and leave without an answer.

Should God commission an angel to come from Glory, if he should honor you and me with his presence and would stand here long enough for me to ask the question of my text, he would turn and wing his way back to the throne of God, fold his wings like a tired dove, and I would stand gazing off into illimitable space without an answer.

There is no escape if you neglect so great salvation.

A. Neglect Means Opportunities Lost That Cannot Return

Sinners who put off trusting Christ cannot escape reaping a harvest of lost opportunities, opportunities of the love of God that will never again return. Every opportunity turned down is an opportunity gone forever. Others *may* come — and they *may not* — but the one ignored will never return to invite you again. Opportunities are like "water spilt on the ground, which cannot be gathered up again" (II Sam. 14:14).

James H. McConkey told of a Scotch botanist who lay one day in a field looking for hours at a heather bell under his microscope. Suddenly, noticing a shadow falling across his glass, he looked up to see a tall, weather-beaten shepherd mirthfully struggling to conceal his amusement over a grown man spending so much time looking at such a common thing as a heather bell.

In defense the botanist merely handed the shepherd the glass and he, too, looked for many enraptured moments. Handing back the glass to the botanist, the latter noted huge tears streaming down the bronzed face of his new acquaintance.

"What's wrong," inquired the botanist, "isn't it beautiful?"

"Oh," replied the subdued shepherd, "of course it is beautiful — beautiful beyond words. *I am just thinking of how many thousands of them I have carelessly trodden under foot in my lifetime!*"

Have you ever stopped to seriously consider how many opportunities to accept Christ you have trodden under in your lifetime? The Bible declares, "behold, now is the accepted time; behold, now is the day of salvation" (II Cor. 6:2). God's opportunity is always *now*. Every tick of the clock presents you with a golden opportunity to trust Christ and be saved. That means you have sixty of God's "nows" every minute of your life, several thousand every hour of every day, over four score thousand every day of every year, many millions in the course of every year, and unnumbered billions of God's "nows" before the normal life span is finished. What will you say when you face the Saviour with those billions of trampled "nows" screaming out the utter justice of your eternal condemnation?

Antonious Felix was faced with God's "now" opportunity as he heard the Spirit-filled apostle present his passionate message of "righteousness, temperance, and judgment to come" (Acts 24:25). The Holy Spirit used the message to stir his soul to the very depths! The consciousness of his sins and the realization of the message's truthfulness caused him to literally tremble with fear and conviction. But Felix foolishly trampled upon that opportunity by replying, "Go thy way for this time; when I have a convenient season, I will call for thee." Historians tell us, however, that the convenient season never came and Felix died in disgraceful suicide just a few years afterward. He was convicted, but not converted; almost persuaded, but altogether lost because he neglected so great salvation. He let his opportunity slip!

King Herod Agrippa is another tragic example of trampling under foot divinely given opportunities of salvation. He, too, heard a Spirit-inspired sermon from the lips of the prince of apostles. He, too, was stirred to the innermost depths of his soul with conviction. But he, too, said "No" with the pitiful lament, "Almost thou persuadest me to be a Christian" (Acts 26:28). Historians tell us that he, too, faded from the political scene an insignificant failure a short time later. Almost persuaded was not sufficient as he foolishly neglected so great salvation. He let his opportunity slip!

Do not, I beg you, make the same fatal mistake! Every lost opportunity draws you closer to the last one and nearer to a permanent home in Hell. Napoleon was wrong about a lot of things, but he was right when he said, "Every moment lost gives an opportunity for misfortune." Delay means death, doom and damnation for the soul apart from Christ. "How shall we escape, if we neglect so great salvation?"

B. Neglect Means No Escape from Misspent, Wasted Life

If you do neglect this wonderful salvation God has provided for sinners, you cannot escape reaping a lost, wasted, misspent life lived serving sin, Satan and the fleeting tinsels of time. You may have many treasures stored up in earthly vaults, but "we brought nothing into this world, and it is certain we can carry nothing out" (I Tim. 6:7). As God reminded the psalmist, "Be not thou afraid when one is made rich, when the glory of his house is increased; For when he dieth he shall carry nothing away: his glory shall not descend after him. Though while he lived he blessed his soul . . ." (Ps. 49:16-18).

If you become a billionaire and die unconverted your life will have been wasted and misspent. The Saviour said, "For what is a man profited, if he shall gain the whole world, and lose his own soul? or what shall a man give in exchange for his soul?" (Matt. 16:26). No matter how high you rise in this life with its successes and triumphs, if you die without Christ it is all loss and no profit! Be not deceived!

But a life of sin is a wasted, misspent life not only in the matter of accomplishment, but from the standpoint of influence as well. Most vividly I recall the pathetic story of a young mother who came to me for counsel a few weeks ago. With bitter tears she told a tragic tale of how she had influenced the high school crowd of girls she ran with into a life of sin. She had taught them to smoke, to lie to their parents, to pet with boys, and other such forms of sinful folly.

With downcast eyes, sometimes with her head buried in her hands in overwhelming grief, she told of sin's bitter payoff to her personally. At home as she talked was her sweet, innocent baby fathered by a man not her husband — and she could not say for certain who he was. In her humiliation she had married another whom she did not love simply to give the baby a name.

Then, to add pain to shame, her health broke in both mind and body to the extent that doctors despaired of her life. Broken in heart, troubled in mind, afflicted in body, despising herself and her sin, she turned to God with earnest, humble repentance and faith. He immediately forgave her and cleansed her, of course! Did not He promise in I John 1:9, "If we confess our sins, he is faithful and just to forgive us our sins, and to cleanse us from all unrighteousness"?

But that was not the end of the story nor the main burden of her grief as she talked to me. She had been going to the various ones she had led into sin and pleading with them to get right with God, only to have them laugh in her face. One, an unmarried girl dating a married man, confessed to her that she thought she was expecting a baby. Another, also unmarried, told her that she had become pregnant and, to escape the shame, had thrown herself down a flight of stairs to cause a miscarriage and murder the unborn child.

With many tears she confessed that she was to blame for leading them into their sin and begged me to tell her how she could undo the wrong and win them to Christ. I couldn't help her much; I don't know that she ever can win them! God in His wonderful grace has forgiven her, but even the grace of the Almighty cannot right the years of her wrong influence.

I recall with sorrow the years of my own sin and rejection of Christ. I did wrong then, especially through my influence in the lives of others, that can never be made right. Some of my companions in sin fell in the Battle of the Bulge, at Normandy, at Iwo Jima, and on other battle fronts during World War II. They are already in Hell and nothing I can do now, nothing even God can do now, can help them!

You are no different from me or this girl I have mentioned. You are scattering your hurtful influence to the four winds, consciously and unconsciously, every day that you live without Christ. Romans 14:7 reminds us all, "For none of us liveth to himself, and no man dieth to himself." Every day of life, and in the day of death as well, our influence is effecting others. If you neglect so great salvation it is impossible to escape reaping a lost, wasted, misspent life.

C. Neglect Means No Escape from a Hardened Heart

Nor can you escape reaping a cold, stony, hardened heart! Delay becomes a disease. Hebrews 3:12, 13, warns, "Take heed, brethren, lest there be in any of you an evil heart of unbelief, in departing from the living God. But exhort one another daily, while it is called To day; lest any of you be hardened through the deceitfulness of sin." Delay gives sin the always accepted opportunity of hardening the sinner's heart against the Gospel.

No one can remain unconverted long and stay tenderhearted. The deceitfulness of sin quickly turns the clay into iron, the water into ice, the putty into rock. The Gospel of Christ is still a twoedged sword (Heb. 4:12) that cuts both ways. Each time it is heard it either turns the sinner's heart toward God or hardens it against God. No sermon preached in the power of the Holy Spirit of God leaves you unaffected or unchanged.

When I was pastor of a church in Long Beach, California, we moved into the Bixby Knolls section of the city, not far from the Long Beach Municipal Airport. It was in the late forties and Uncle Sam's Air Force was just beginning to develop a strong fleet of jet fighter planes. When the wind was out of the northwest they would take off directly over our house.

I will never forget the first time a jet flew over after we had moved in. We were at the dinner table when suddenly a tremendous vibrating roar shook the entire house and for all the world it sounded as if a plane were about to crash into our dwelling. We jumped from the table and ran to the yard just in time to see the jet passing directly over our house, just a few hundred feet above us.

The next few times the wind was in the direction necessitating a takeoff over our house we jumped again in fear, but eventually we became so accustomed to it that we paid no attention at all. We were safe. One would never crash into *our* house.

But some time after we left Long Beach one *did* crash into a house in that immediate vicinity, killing several people. No doubt their reaction had been the same as ours: first, tremendous alarm and fear; second, a gradual process of becoming accustomed to the roar of the jets; until, finally, they felt perfectly secure and free from danger. *Then destruction struck in one mad moment excluding all escape!*

Sin is like that! Many a man has been stirred with a deep conviction he felt he could not ignore. Both his head and his heart urged him to settle the matter of his soul's salvation immediately, only to have him neglect his decision until sudden destruction had struck. Thousands who once trembled with fear during gospel invitations now stand serenely smiling while the preacher pleads.

I just closed a meeting in Kansas where an unsaved husband came to hear me preach more faithfully than many of the church members. Old-timers told me how he used to stand weeping, gripping the pew in front of him in visible agony during an evangelistic invitation. Now he appears, outwardly at least, not to have the slightest concern about his soul. As a matter of fact, it seemed that he was almost sneering while I begged the lost to get right with God.

Had he crossed the deadline? I do not know, of course, but I doubt it since he came so regularly to hear me preach. I do know that his heart had become hardened through the deceitfulness of sin to such an extent that he will probably continue his sin and rejection of Christ until he lands in Hell. *Every day you remain away from God increases the probability you will be lost forever!*

I have before me as I write these lines a letter just received from a missionary in far-off South India. In telling of the work with a spirit-worshiping tribe of aborigines, this missionary says, "They beg us to tell them more and more, until our throats are so tired we can hardly speak another word. We pray for others to come to help us . . ."

Here is a strange thing! Idolatrous heathen in a far-off country beg the few missionaries in that land to tell the gospel message until their throats are so raw and tired they can speak no more. Yet cultured, refined, educated Americans pay scant attention to the familiar story of Jesus and His love. What makes the difference? The answer, in the language of our text, is continued sin and repeated rejection. The heathen of India has not had his heart hardened from hearing the Gospel over and over again. On the other hand, the American without Christ has had thousands of opportunities to be saved — *and spurned them all!* His heart has become hardened, calloused, indifferent, unconcerned and unmoved.

Don't you see your danger? Your repeated failures to trust Christ are hardening your heart and sealing your doom! ". . . hardened through the deceitfulness of sin!" "How shall we escape, if we neglect so great salvation?"

Historians tell us that Aaron Burr was ready to give his heart to Christ one night in a revival meeting at his college town. He started to go forward during the invitation, but just as he was about to step into the aisle Satan suggested that he wait and get the advice of the president of Princeton University first. He did.

The foolish president advised him to wait until the meeting was over, until the excitement, emotionalism and enthusiasm had died and then, if he still felt moved to do so, trust Christ. He accepted that advice, but when the meeting was over, when the emotionalism and enthusiasm had died down, he found he no longer had any desire to even consider the claims of Christ. So Aaron Burr went on in his sin and we have good reason to believe is in Hell as a Christ-rejecter today because he "put off," he neglected so great salvation.

I beg you, do not follow in Aaron Burr's footsteps. Do not delay accepting Jesus Christ as your personal Saviour. Hebrews 3:7, 8, admonishes, "Wherefore (as the Holy Ghost saith, To day if ye will hear his voice, Harden not your hearts . . .)" If you *do* delay you cannot escape reaping a cold, stony, hardened, deadened heart.

D. *How Can You Escape Hell If You Neglect?*

Finally, if you neglect this so great salvation you cannot escape reaping a lost soul, sentenced to eternal torment in Hell. Galatians 6:7, 8 declares, "Be not deceived; God is not mocked: for whatsoever a man soweth, that shall he also reap. For he that soweth to his flesh shall of the flesh reap corruption; but he that soweth to the Spirit shall of the Spirit reap life everlasting."

Hebrews 10:26-31 adds this warning:

> For if we sin wilfully after that we have received the knowledge of the truth, there remaineth no more sacrifice for sins, But a certain fearful looking for of judgment and fiery indignation, which shall devour the adversaries. He that despised Moses' law died without mercy under two or three witnesses: Of how much sorer punishment, suppose ye, shall he be thought worthy, who hath trodden under foot the Son of God, and hath counted the blood of the covenant, wherewith he was sanctified, an unholy thing, and hath done despite unto the Spirit of grace? For we know him that hath said, Vengeance belongeth unto me, I will

recompence, saith the Lord. And again, The Lord shall judge his people. It is a fearful thing to fall into the hands of the living God.

It is still true that folks who expect to claim salvation at the eleventh hour usually die at ten-thirty. Postponement is persistently perilous! Proverbs 27:1 warns, "Boast not thyself of to morrow; for thou knowest not what a day may bring forth." And Proverbs 29:1 makes the matter even more urgent when it says, "He, that being often reproved hardeneth his neck, shall suddenly be destroyed, and that without remedy."

Years ago a corps of civil engineers repeatedly warned the inhabitants of a little Pennsylvania village that the dam above them in the mountains was unsafe, that they should flee from the village before it broke. But at every warning they only laughed and mocked. With sneers, their only reply was, *"You can't scare us!"*

Fifteen days after the last warning, the dam broke, sixteen million tons of water from the Conemaugh Lake reservoir came roaring down the valley, like "ceaseless peals of thunder," and within thirty minutes after it struck the town, Johnstown, Pennsylvania, was in ruins with over 2,700 of its inhabitants hurled into the presence of God.

You, too, have been warned many times of your dangerous condition outside of Christ. Oh, do not foolishly follow that philosophy and come to the fate of those who say, *"You can't scare me!"* You *know* the Bible is true! You *know* that you are a sinner! You *know* that Christ is your only hope! *Then trust Him today!* Fall at His feet in faith before it is forever too late! Get right with God while you still have the opportunity.

Isaiah 55:6, 7 invites with a warning, "Seek ye the Lord while he may be found, call ye upon him while he is near: Let the wicked forsake his way, and the unrighteous man his thoughts: and let him return unto the Lord, and he will have mercy upon him; and to our God, for he will abundantly pardon." II Corinthians 6:2 says, ". . . behold, now is the accepted time; behold, now is the day of salvation."

Do not say, in the words of a song of yesteryear, "I'll Be Saved, But Not Tonight!" Penned by an unknown writer, it tells the tragic story of multitudes in our day:

Come, poor sinner, seek salvation, Jesus waits to put you right;
Do not give that dreadful answer, "I'll be saved, but not tonight;
Give me just a little longer, for this world seems, oh! so bright,
When I feel that I am dying, I'll be saved, but not tonight."

Oh, how vain is the delusion that the Lord your time will wait,
Millions now are lost forever, shut without the Golden Gate;
Once the Saviour spake and bade them enter in His perfect light;
But, like you, they answered softly, "I'll be saved, but not tonight."

When the Judgment overtakes you, how those words will stand in
sight,
When they prayed and pleaded with you, and you answered, "Not
tonight";
Then will be the time, my brother, when you stand at death's cold
brink,
When your soul is lost forever, without Christ you're sure to sink.

Look again at the first verse of our text: "Therefore we ought
to give the more earnest heed to the things which we have heard,
lest at any time we should let them slip." Dear friend, *don't let
this warning slip!* Repent of your sins and accept Jesus Christ
as your Saviour, *right now!*

I began this message with the story of a man overboard; let
me close it with another. A sailor on a ship called the *Cunarder*
was working high on the mast when suddenly he lost his hold,
falling to the sea below. Immediately that chilling cry was
sounded, "Man overboard! Man overboard!" Soon a lifeline
had been thrown him, he had grasped it and strong hands had
pulled him to the deck of the ship.

For a long time he remained stretched out on the deck while
doctors and companions worked over him. His eyes were open
and occasionally his lips moved without sound, but they could
not get him to let loose of the lifeline. Finally, after considerable
time had elapsed, he managed to whisper, "Captain, I can't
let go; I gripped it for my life!" And it was four more hours
before the muscles in his arms and fingers had relaxed sufficiently
for him to let loose of that lifeline.

That sailor was no fool! About to die a horrible death of
drowning, he saw within his reach a lifeline that could save
him and he grasped it with all the strength he had within him.

Are you as wise as he in a far more serious and important matter, the salvation of your eternal soul?

You are drowning in the sea of sin, sinking into the dreadful fate of an eternal death in Hell. I am offering — yea, God is offering you through His Word — a lifeline called salvation. Will you grasp it? John 1:12 promises, "But as many as received him, to them gave he power to become the sons of God, even to them that believe on his name." Will you receive Him? Will you believe on His name?

"How shall we escape, if we neglect so great salvation?"

DECISION FOR CHRIST

If you are willing to end your neglect and rejection of the lovely Lord today will you sign the decision form below, then copy it in a letter to me or write me in your own words what you have done? I will be thrilled to know of your conversion and will write you a letter of counsel and instruction about how to live for Christ.

Evangelist Robert L. Sumner
P. O. Box 157
Brownsburg, Indiana 46112

Dear Brother Sumner:

I have just read your sermon, "Slipping into Hell." I fully realize now that by my neglect I have been sinning grievously against the Lord and deserve His punishment in an eternal Hell. However, if Jesus Christ is willing to receive me, I am willing to receive Him without any more delay. Right now, the best I know how, I repent of my sins and trust Christ to save me. I honestly want to live for Him and do what He wants me to do. This very moment I do trust Him to make me a son of God.

Signed --

Address ---

4

HAVE YOU COUNTED THE COST?

> For what is a man profited, if he shall gain the whole world, and lose his own soul? or what shall a man give in exchange for his soul?
>
> For the Son of man shall come in the glory of his Father with his angels; and then he shall reward every man according to his works (Matt. 16:26, 27).

Have you ever earnestly, seriously, soberly sought to determine the true value of your soul? Have you ever considered its real worth in the light of an eternal existence either in a glorious Heaven or a terrible Hell? *Just what is a soul worth?*

A few years ago I witnessed the futile attempt to liberate beautiful, blond, three-year-old Kathy Fiscus, who had fallen some 96 feet into an abandoned well at San Marino, California. Within 45 minutes after her plight became known, volunteer firemen were pumping air by hand into the narrow well and continued unceasingly for nearly 50 hours. Drillers, sand hogs, hardrock miners, engineers and others risked their lives and labored without rest until, in some instances, they dropped from utter exhaustion and fatigue. According to one Long Beach, California, newspaper, machinery, tools, equipment and material were used which would have cost over a quarter of a million dollars if the rescue had been conducted on a commercial basis.

The whole world was so upset and excited it could hardly wait for news. Leading newspapers in Stockholm, London, Australia, and other major points around the globe held their presses for last minute news of Kathy! Switchboards at newspaper offices and radio stations everywhere were jammed with calls from the moment her plight first become known. In Chicago it brought the greatest number of phone calls to that city's newspapers since the end of World War II. The *Dallas News* said it got a "jillion" calls. The *Salt Lake City Tribune,* the *Minneapolis Tribune,* the *Pittsburgh Post-Gazette,* and the *Philadelphia Inquirer* were among the leading newspapers across the nation reporting unusual incidents and multiplied calls.

Advice came from everywhere! Suggestions ranged from Chicago Fire Marshal Anthony J. Mullaney's telegram: "Try everything. Nothing is too silly or impossible with this girl's life at stake," to a six-year-old's message from Portland, Oregon: "If Kathy could read, I'd send her my magic book and she'd get out quick." Bystanders were urged to contribute any idea, "no matter how silly it sounds." Midgets, circus thin men, contortionists, plumbers, sand hogs, jockeys, and others by the hundreds volunteered to attempt a descent into the 14-inch pipe in which she was wedged.

Ten thousand people were on the scene watching and hundreds of thousands more refused to budge from radio and television sets. This heart-moving human interest drama became the scene of the first uninterrupted twenty-four hour television broadcast in world history. Over 500 people were reported standing around one automobile listening to the radio account of the rescue attempt. A radio news bulletin over KNX stated that Los Angeles theaters grossed their lowest amount in years as people remained at home by radios and televisions to get the latest word on developments. Churches throughout the area were virtually deserted that Sunday night. A rescue fund was started for the workers which finally totaled over forty-two thousands dollars and was shared by one hundred and thirty-two men.

Yet, in spite of the heroic efforts of unrelenting workers, at 8:58 Sunday night, after more than 50 hours of continuous labor, Dr. Paul Hanson announced to the waiting world that Kathy Fiscus was *dead,* and *had been dead since before the rescue started.*

Think of it, dear reader, all of this time, effort and expense put forth for a little life which passed straight into the arms of Jesus the very moment her tiny heart stopped beating. Please do not misunderstand me; I do not begrudge one penny of money or one moment of time spent in that rescue attempt — if it had been one of my little girls instead of Kathy, I would not have wanted one whit less — but I *do* want to impress upon you the thought that if a *life* is worth that much, how exceedingly valuable must be that of a *soul!* Your soul, Jesus said, is worth more than the world and all the fullness thereof.

In every transaction of life the paramount issue is: "*What'll it cost?*" This is true when the real estate agent shows you a home, when the salesman shows you a car, when the clerk brings out a suit or a dress which pleases your eye. Those who have been rejecting the Saviour ought to solemnly ask themselves: "What will it cost?" and then set out to determine the true Bible answer. In the words of A. J. Hodge's haunting hymn:

> There's a line that is drawn by rejecting our Lord,
> Where the call of His Spirit is lost,
> And you hurry along with the pleasure-mad throng—
> Have you counted, have you counted the cost?
>
> You may barter your hope of eternity's morn,
> For a moment of joy at the most,
> For the glitter of sin and the things it will win—
> Have you counted, have you counted the cost?
>
> While the door of His mercy is open to you,
> Ere the depth of His love you exhaust,
> Won't you come and be healed, won't you whisper, I yield —
> I have counted, I have counted the cost?
>
> Have you counted the cost, if your soul should be lost,
> Tho' you gain the whole world for your own?
> Even now it may be that the line you have crossed,
> Have you counted, have you counted the cost?

The Lord Jesus Christ, in our text, was seeking to drive home to the hearts of men the truth that *it costs more to be lost* than to be saved. In the two previous verses He had described the price of discipleship with the words: "If any man will come after me, let him deny himself, and take up his cross, and follow me. For whosoever will save his life shall lose it: and whosoever will lose his life for my sake shall find it." Yes, all-out discipleship, following Jesus fully, *costs something!* I wouldn't want it any other way, would you? Don't you feel as David expressed it in II Samuel 24:24, "Neither will I offer . . . unto the Lord my God of that which doth cost me nothing"?

Our Lord did not describe discipleship as a bed of roses. He declared in John 15:18-20: "If the world hate you, ye know that it hated me before it hated you. If ye were of the world, the world would love his own: but because ye are not of the world, but I have chosen you out of the world, therefore the world hateth you. Remember the word that I said unto you, The servant is not greater than his lord. If they have persecuted me, they will also persecute you; if they have kept my saying, they will keep yours also."

Paul intimated the same when he said, "Thou therefore endure hardness, as a good soldier of Jesus Christ. No man that warreth entangleth himself with the affairs of this life; that he may please him who hath chosen him to be a soldier" (II Tim. 2:3, 4).

Yes, true discipleship costs something! But our gracious Lord wanted to press home the truth: *It costs more to be lost!* Proverbs 13:15 is still the dictum of both experience and revelation: "Good understanding giveth favour: but the way of transgressors is hard!"

The most terrible transgression, the greatest sin, is that of rejecting God's salvation as set forth in His Word. Nothing else, be it murder, rape, robbery, profanity, adultery, or some other sin, is as wicked when weighed in the divine balances of Glory. To prove this charge against mankind, consider again

I. THE CONDEMNING CRIME

The Scripture says, "He that believeth on him is not condemned: but he that believeth not is condemned already" (John 3:18). The Christ-rejecting sinner is condemned for fighting God, crucifying Christ and scorning the sweet Holy Spirit.

A. *The Sin of Fighting the Father*

The Bible calls this the crime of *fighting the Father!* James 4:4 declares: "Ye adulterers and adulteresses, know ye not that the friendship of the world is enmity with God? whosoever therefore will be a friend of the world is the enemy of God." In other words, if you are not *for* Him, you are *against* Him! There is no neutral ground, no sitting on the fence. Indifference is defiance! Oh, that every wayward wanderer could see and realize that friendship with the world, pursuit of pleasure, spurning the Bible way, is simply warfare against Almighty God!

The second chapter of Ephesians uses such terms as "enmity," "wall of partition," "afar off," "strangers," "aliens," and "foreigners" in describing this condition of the unsaved man. One of the hottest lies out of Hell is that all men have a "spark of divinity" within their breasts which needs only to be "fanned into flame." The same second chapter of Ephesians describes unsaved men as "children of disobedience" and "children of wrath" who pattern their lives after the dictates of the devil!

This act of fighting the Father is not necessarily a Bolshevik program of seeking to dethrone Him. It may merely find its outlet in seeking wealth, pleasure, fame, success, honor or other worldly baubles and *forgetting God*. Think of it: *forgetting God!*

A few miles from where I formerly pastored, at Camp Wolters, Texas, two privates of the same platoon sat on their bunks talking. They had both been inducted at Fort Sheridan, Illinois, and for two months had been eating, sleeping and training together. In the course of their conversation that afternoon they discovered that one was from 2541 South Troy Street, Chicago, and the other from 2553 South Troy Street in the same windy city. It turned out that they had been close neighbors—on the same side of the street — for thirteen years, but had been total strangers to one another until they became acquainted so far from home. More amazing than this, however, is the truth that men walk God's earth, eat His food, breathe His air, live by His power and profit by His blessings, only to remain total strangers to Him and whose only contact is that of rebellion and rejection!

B. *It Is the Crime of Crucifying Christ*

But that is not all! This condemning crime is also one of *crucifying the Christ!* Hebrews 6:6, speaking of the fully enlightened sinner who turns down Christ and goes back to his sin, says, ". . . they crucify to themselves the Son of God afresh, and put him to an open shame." When men turn down Christ they do not literally crucify Him again — that was done "once for all" (Heb. 10:10, 12, 14); but they are signifying their approval of what was done and indicating they would have done the same if given the opportunity. Your rejection of God's salvation is a public manifestation that you would rather *kill* Christ than *crown* Him!

The guilt of "Christ-killing" is more than Pilate's! Remember how he washed his hands in that basin of water and sought to free himself from the responsibility of Christ's death. *He failed!* On the books of Heaven the crime is laid to his account. In like manner, men today try to escape responsibility, but like Pilate, they, too, fail in the eyes of God.

The guilt of "Christ-killing" is more than Judas'. How the world looks upon him with scorn, shame and contempt! Even the Jews who paid him off had no respect for a man who would stoop so low. Yet, in the eyes of God, if you are rejecting Jesus Christ as your personal Saviour, you are as guilty as he! His guilt is your guilt!

Yes, the guilt of "Christ-killing" is more than the Temple Jews', more than the Roman soldiers', more than Herod's, more than the howling mob's, more than the easily swayed multitude's.

Dear friend out of Christ, this guilt of "Christ-killing" *is yours!* It is yours, first, because *your* sins nailed Him to the Cross. He was wounded for *your* transgressions; He was bruised for *your* iniquities. It is yours, second, because your rejection is your vote for His death!

One of the most bitter statements in all the Bible to me is that found in Mark 14:64: "Ye have heard the blasphemy: what think ye? And they all condemned him to be guilty of death." With a unanimous vote, every ballot was marked, "Guilty of death." In a figurative sense, sinners today are sitting at that council table casting their votes by their actions.

How are you voting, *for* or *against* Jesus Christ? Remember that the Lord declared in Matthew 12:30, "He that is not with me is against me; and he that gathereth not with me scattereth abroad." There is no neutral ground!

C. *The Sin of Insulting the Holy Spirit*

But even more than fighting the Father and crucifying the Christ, this crime of refusing God's way of salvation is described as *scorning the Spirit.* Hebrews 10:29 says: "Of how much sorer punishment, suppose ye, shall he be thought worthy, who hath trodden under foot the Son of God, and hath counted the blood of the covenant, wherewith he was sanctified, an unholy thing, and hath done despite unto the Spirit of grace?" The word "despite" literally means "insult" and is descriptive of what happens when a man rejects God's salvation — he insults the Spirit of God, called here the Spirit of Grace.

The Holy Spirit is the Special Messenger inviting you to salvation and eternal life. Jesus, speaking of His ministry, said in John 16:8-11: "And when he is come, he will reprove the world of sin, and of righteousness, and of judgment: Of sin, because they believe not on me; Of righteousness, because I go to my Father, and ye see me no more; Of judgment, because the prince of this world is judged."

The Holy Spirit invites you to receive forgiveness of sins, and you say, "I pray thee have me excused" (Luke 14:18). He invites you to exchange Hell for Heaven as your eternal home, and you say, "I pray thee have me excused!" He beseeches you to enter into a life of peace, happiness and fullness of joy, and you say, "I pray thee have me excused!" He invites you to share the privilege of walking down the streets of Glory with loved ones already on the other side, and you say, "I pray thee have me excused!" Rejecting salvation is scorning and insulting God's Spirit.

> As you seek for the pleasures that soon pass away,
> Have you e'er stopped to think of the cost?
> Have you valued your soul 'gainst the things that decay,
> Have you counted the terrible cost?
>
> As the voice of the Spirit you strive to forget,
> And His pleadings aside you have toss'd,
> Have you tho't when you said, "There is time enough yet,"
> What it means, what it means to be lost?
>
> If you gain all the world, drink from fortune's rich bowl,
> And in judgment your soul should be lost,
> Then what price can you give in exchange for your soul?
> You will wish you had counted the cost.

Have you counted the cost, the unspeakable cost,
Is it worth such a price to be lost?
For the joys that will fade shall your soul be betrayed,
Have you counted, have you counted the cost?

Let us consider now

II. THE CONSEQUENT COST

of this condemning crime!

A. The Heavy Price of a Wasted Life

For one thing, there is the cost of a wasted life! If you continue on unsaved your life will be wasted in the sense of ruin. Galatians 6:7 testifies, "Be not deceived; God is not mocked: for whatsoever a man soweth, that shall he also reap."

Numbers 32:23 insists, "But if ye will not do so, behold, ye have sinned against the Lord: and be sure your sin will find you out."

Job 4:8 contains this observation, "Even as I have seen, they that plow iniquity, and sow wickedness, reap the same."

Make no mistake about it, dear friend, if you reject Christ you are sure to reap a wrecked, wasted, ruined life. Spiritual laws of sowing and reaping insist that they who sow to the wind must reap the whirlwind.

Not long ago in a Texas jail I won a young husband and father to Christ who had been arrested for the rape of a junior high school girl. He had picked her up, gone to the county line for beer, had drunk until reason had fled, then committed the dastardly deed. In jail, broken-hearted, he was easy to win and today he is studying his Bible and doing correspondence work at the Huntsville state prison.

However, never will I forget my last visit to his cell before he went on trial for that crime capable of producing the sentence of death! Over and over I have wished it might have been possible for every young person in the world to have been with me at that hour and heard his testimony. That Sunday, as I concluded reading, praying and talking with him, I turned to leave his cell block only to have him reach through the bars, grip my arm and plead, "Don't go! Please don't go! Please stay and talk with me just a little bit longer!" He was trembling from head to foot, his voice was shaking and his eyes bulged from their sockets in pathetic pleading. He said, "Sit down there on the radiator by the window and talk to me." When I hesitated, he grabbed a blanket from his cot and said, "Here! Sit on this! I don't want you to go. I want you to talk to me just a little bit longer." Of course I stayed a few more minutes and counseled him some more from the Scripture, but for days after his words and his actions haunted my memory. *His sin had found him out!* The devil was picking up an installment payment on his wasted life!

Not only is a life lived without Christ wasted in the sense of ruin, but also in the sense of accomplishments. Your life will be a failure if you reject Christ, regardless of how many earthly successes, gains, honors or triumphs are yours.

I Timothy 6:7 reminds us: "For we brought nothing into this world, and it is certain we can carry nothing out." And Psalm 49:17 adds: "For when he dieth he shall carry nothing away: his glory shall not descend after him."

If you make a million dollars and die unsaved, *you will die a failure!* If you become the President of the United States or the dictator of the world and die without Christ, *you will stand in the presence of God a total failure.* If you drink the cup of this world's pleasures to the very dregs, yet die a lost soul, *you will face the judgment bar of God an unavailing, hopeless, bankrupt sinner awaiting only the sentence of eternal doom!*

The cost of rebellion and rejection is the cost of a life wasted and ruined and worthless!

B. The Cost of a Broken Heart

Next, the consequent cost of turning down God's "so great salvation" is the price of a broken heart. I use the term "broken heart" in the sense of someone seeking something, only to discover when they have obtained it that it is a sham, a farce and a disillusionment.

Sin is like that! Those who have tried it have found it wanting. Men can drink of everything that this world has to offer and never find satisfaction. Jeremiah 2:13 describes the best the world can give with the words: "My people have committed two evils; they have forsaken me the fountain of living waters, and hewed them out cisterns, broken cisterns, that can hold no water."

Dear reader, real satisfaction is found only in Christ. He said in John 4:14, "But whosoever drinketh of the water that I shall give him shall never thirst; but the water that I shall give him shall be in him a well of water springing up into everlasting life."

King Solomon's experience bears out the truth that "vanity" is all that this world can produce, never satisfaction. His testimony is found in the second chapter of Ecclesiastes and recorded for the profit of all who are wise enough to be willing to learn from the experience of others.

Pleasure failed to satisfy! He wrote, "I said in mine heart, Go to now, I will prove thee with mirth, therefore enjoy pleasure: and, behold, this also is vanity. I said of laughter, It is mad: and of mirth, What doeth it?" (vv. 1, 2).

Strong drink failed to satisfy! He wrote, "I sought in mine heart to give myself unto wine, yet acquainting mine heart with wisdom; and to lay hold on folly, till I might see what was that good for the sons of men, which they should do under the heaven all the days of their life" (v. 3).

Great achievements failed to satisfy! He wrote,

> I made me great works; I builded me houses; I planted me vineyards: I made me gardens and orchards, and I planted trees in them of all kind of fruits: I made me pools of water, to water therewith the wood that bringeth forth trees. . . . Then I looked on all the works that my hands had wrought, and on the labour that I had laboured to do: and, behold, all was vanity and vexation of spirit, and there was no profit under the sun. . . . Yea, I hated all my labour which I had taken under the sun: because I should leave it unto the man that shall be after me (vv. 4-6, 11, 18).

Was it not Alexander the Great who sat down and wept, after conquering the known world, because there were no more worlds to conquer? Achievements do not satisfy and even if they did, as Solomon said, they would only be left "unto the man that shall be after me."

Wealth failed to satisfy! Again he wrote,

> I gathered me also silver and gold, and the peculiar treasure of kings and of the provinces: I gat me men singers and women

singers, and the delights of the sons of men, as musical instruments, and that of all sorts. So I was great, and increased more than all that were before me in Jerusalem: also my wisdom remained with me. And whatsoever mine eyes desired I kept not from them, I withheld not my heart from any joy; for my heart rejoiced in all my labour: and this was my portion of all my labour . . . and, behold, all was vanity and vexation of spirit, and there was no profit under the sun (vv. 8-10, 11c).

No wonder Fanny Crosby so sweetly carolled:

> Take the world, but give me Jesus,
> All its joys are but a name;
> But His love abideth ever,
> Thro' eternal years the same!

C. *The Decision against Christ Costs a Damning Influence*

Another consequent cost of a life lived apart from Jesus Christ is the cost of a damning influence. Romans 14:7 well says, "For none of us liveth to himself, and no man dieth to himself." It is impossible to live or die without influencing, for good or bad, the lives of others. If you are unsaved, your influence can only be for unrighteousness, for Satan, for Hell, for sin, for lawlessness, for rebellion and rejection of Christ. It is impossible to influence others for Heaven unless you are on the road to Heaven yourself. It is impossible to influence others for holiness unless your life is a pattern of righteousness and purity.

Where is *your* influence? Especially is this influence strong in the case of parents over children, husbands over wives, wives over husbands, and teachers over pupils.

Our Lord made a tremendous charge in Luke 11:52 when He said, "Woe unto you, lawyers! for ye have taken away the key of knowledge: ye entered not in yourselves, and them that were entering in ye hindered!" What guilt could be greater than that of "hindering" another soul from salvation and Heaven? Yet that is exactly what you are doing every day you continue traveling down the broad road in rejection of Jesus Christ.

D. *The Eternal, Immeasurable Loss of Your Soul*

After all, the main cost for you in refusing salvation is not a wasted life, not a broken heart, not a damning influence; the main consequent cost for you is a lost soul! If you gain the world, but lose your soul, it will be all loss and no profit!

Once again I ask the question set forth at the start of the message: *Just what is your soul worth?* Jesus declared it was worth more than all the world and to prove it He went all the way to Calvary's blood-stained tree to redeem it! In view of the beaten, battered, broken body, the poured-out blood, the mental, spiritual, physical suffering and anguish, the very heart-break of God, your soul is worth too much to be lost! The sufferings of the Son of God help us to see the worth of a soul!

Don't you see how foolish, how fatal, it is to go on without Him? Jesus said that if you gained the world but lost your soul, it would be a bad bargain, impossible to better throughout a long eternity. Certainly you must realize that you cannot gain the world, but, thank God, you can gain the Saviour! In the words of Swedish Anna Olander:

> If I gained the world, but lost the Saviour,
> Were my life worth living for a day?
> Could my yearning heart find rest and comfort
> In the things that soon must pass away?
> If I gained the world, but lost the Saviour,
> Would my gain be worth the life-long strife?
> Are all earthly pleasures worth comparing
> For a moment with a Christ-filled life?
>
> Had I wealth and love in fullest measure,
> And a name revered both far and near,
> Yet no hope beyond, no harbor waiting,
> Where my storm-tossed vessel I could steer;
> If I gained the world, but lost the Saviour,
> Who endured the cross and died for me,
> Could then all the world afford a refuge,
> Whither, in my anguish, I might flee?
>
> O what emptiness! without the Saviour
> 'Mid the sins and sorrows here below!
> And eternity, how dark without Him!
> Only night and tears and endless woe!
> What, tho' I might live without the Saviour,
> When I come to die, how would it be?
> O to face the valley's gloom without Him!
> And without Him all eternity!

> O the joy of having all in Jesus!
> What a balm the broken heart to heal!
> Ne'er a sin so great, but He'll forgive it,
> Nor a sorrow that He does not feel!
> If I have but Jesus, only Jesus,
> Nothing else in all the world beside,
> O then ev'rything is mine in Jesus;
> For my needs and more He will provide.

Will you not, dear friend, right now lay all your rebellion down and receive the sweet Saviour as your Lord and Master? II Corinthians 6:2 declares: "For he saith, I have heard thee in a time accepted, and in the day of salvation have I succoured thee: behold, now is the accepted time; behold, now is the day of salvation."

Don't be a "neglector." It has been my observation that those who neglect and delay during life usually continue to neglect and delay during death!

Near the close of my Texas pastorate I received an urgent call from the local hospital to come at once. A man had been shot down in cold blood at one of the city cafes and his relatives, strangers in the city, had asked the hospital to get a minister to talk to him about his soul before he died.

The hospital authorities called me and I went to his bedside, took his hand in mine, leaned over the bed and whispered to him the sweet old story of Jesus and His love. Over and over I softly quoted Romans 10:13, "For whosoever shall call upon the name of the Lord shall be saved," and urged him to call upon this wonderful Lord for salvation. But that white-haired man, oxygen tube up his nose, fighting for breath, with three bullets in his body, standing on the very threshold of eternity, slowly shook his head and said, "No, not now. Perhaps later, but not now. Not now!" Nothing I could say would change his attitude and in a matter of hours he was gone. He had delayed in life and he delayed, too late, in death!

In Arcanum, Ohio, I went at the request of a burdened loved one to visit an unsaved man who was dying of cancer. He was most cordial as I sat across from his thin, pain-wracked body until I began to talk about his need of salvation. Immediately he picked up a newspaper and started reading, completely ignoring my pleas about his soul. When I bowed my head to pray aloud in his behalf, that man in his seventies who was about to face God rattled the newspaper to let me know he was not praying with me or even being reverent while I talked to the Almighty.

In Lansing, Michigan, I went to a hospital to talk with another man in his seventies who was dying of cancer and pneumonia. His son had journeyed all the way from Texas, where he was attending a Bible school, to try to win him to Christ before he died. When I talked to him about the Saviour, he listened for a few moments, then said, "I'm going to wait until next Sunday when all my family will be here." When I gently reminded him he might not have until Sunday and urged him to trust Christ immediately, he gripped the bed sheet with his fist and, with a great deal of pain and effort, slowly pulled himself over on his side, facing the wall, his back to me, indicating the interview was at an end. He did not live until Sunday and he died without the Saviour, sinking immediately into the eternal Hell of unending torment. Yes, long experience has taught me that folks who delay in life usually delay in death, too.

Don't you make the same fatal mistake! Turn this moment to the compassionate Christ who loves you, who will lift you, who will loose you, and who will live in you for ever! Count the cost! "Believe on the Lord Jesus Christ, and thou shalt be saved, and thy house" (Acts 16:31).

DON'T SELL YOUR SOUL; BE SAVED TODAY!

I trust that many a poor sinnner who reads this message now realizes how foolish and wicked it is to go on against God, rejecting the Saviour, letting his soul be damned forever! In Jesus' Name, now, the author begs you to turn to Jesus Christ and trust Him today as your Saviour.

Will you today turn from your sin of fighting God, your sin of crucifying Christ, your sin of insulting the Holy Spirit? Will you repent of your sin and turn to Christ to beg His mercy and trust Him for salvation? The very moment you honestly, with all your heart, turn to believe on Christ, rely upon Him, depend upon Him to save your soul, and give Him your heart, that moment you will be saved. Do not lose your soul! Decide for Christ today.

If you will say an all-out *yes* to Christ today, please sign the decision form below, copy it in a letter, and mail to the author at once. I will rejoice and will send you a letter of counsel and encouragement.

Evangelist Robert L. Sumner
P. O. Box 157
Brownsburg, Indiana 46112

Dear Brother Sumner:

Yes, I have read the sermon, "Have You Counted the Cost?" I realize that I am a poor lost sinner, that I have been fighting against God, crucifying Christ in my heart, and resisting and insulting the Holy Spirit. But I realize if I lose my soul, I lose everything important for eternity. I am sorry for my sin. So here and now I turn from my sin, I turn to Christ for mercy. This moment I trust Him to forgive my sins and save my soul as He promised to do in John 3:16. I claim Christ as my Saviour and will set out to live for Him from this day forth.

Signed _____

Address _____

_____

5

DO YOU THINK YOU WILL GO TO HEAVEN
WHEN YOU DIE?

In my Father's house are many mansions: if it were not so,
I would have told you. I go to prepare a place for you.

And if I go and prepare a place for you, I will come again,
and receive you unto myself; that where I am, there ye may
be also.

And whither I go ye know, and the way ye know.

Thomas saith unto him, Lord, we know not whither thou
goest; and how can we know the way?

Jesus saith unto him, I am the way, the truth, and the life:
no man cometh unto the Father, but by me (John 14:2-6).

While in a crusade for Christ recently at the First Baptist
Church in Warren, Maine, the pastor gave me an interesting
and enlightening clipping he had taken from the *New York
Daily News.* It was the column of the *News'* "Inquiring Fo-
tographer," Jimmy Jemail, who had that day asked six people
on the sidewalks of New York the question: *"Do you think
you will go to Heaven when you die?"*

The first one, a film company representative, answered dog-
matically: "Yes. I am sure of it. There must be justice in its
true sense. Otherwise there would be no logic to living. Going
to Heaven when I die will be but a small recompense for all
the dirty deals, yes, I mean dirty deals, that have come my
way and made life a hell on earth."

This man's hope for Heaven was grounded upon "justice";
but where is justice in overlooking sin, in ignoring the multitudinous transgressions of a normal sinner's life, in letting the
unredeemed wicked join in the same glorious Heaven with
sinners made righteous through the blood of Christ? Note also

his evidence to support his claim of deserving Heaven. He speaks of "dirty deals" and a "hell on earth," but the Bible nowhere offers a single line of Scriptural hope for gaining Heaven through suffering mistreatment at the hands of fellow men. Such abuse, whether real or fancied, will not atone for the awful sin of mistreatment in rejecting the dear Saviour, Jesus Christ!

This Hollywoodite further showed his lack of spiritual understanding when he said, "Going to Heaven when I die will be *but a small recompense. . . .*" What does he think Heaven is, I wonder? Heaven to him will be just a small payment of what God owes him because men have supposedly given him "dirty deals"!

The second one interviewed, a bar maid, said: "I don't know. Like most women, I gossip, talk about others behind their backs, and I'm envious and jealous of other women who have more than I. The only thing I wouldn't do that many women do is go out with a married man. Recently I read a book, *The Devil Is a Woman,* and it made sense. Will I go to Heaven?"

This admission, "I don't know," was the most honest answer given by any of the six interviewed. Noteworthy is the fact that this honky-tonk woman realizes gossip, envy, jealousy, back-biting and other acts of "respectable" people are *terrible sins in the sight of Almighty God!* Yet, in spite of the fact that she does everything in the book but go out with married men, this bar maid seems to think she has a good chance to spend eternity in God's House!

The third one interviewed, an owner of a bar and grill, declared boldly: "Yes, indeed, just as sure as the good Lord has mercy in His heart. I'm going through hell now. I was forced out of my old place of business, where I had been for years. It's hard for my customers to become accustomed to my new place. I've always tried to do the right thing, and there must be some reward."

Like the first man, he is "sure" because he is "going through hell now." However, while the first man claimed "justice," this one claims "mercy" for the same identical reason! In all fairness, though, note that this man crying "mercy" at the start closes by pleading "some reward," *or merit,* the direct opposite of mercy!

Why does this saloon-keeper feel he is entitled to Heaven? Because he had been forced out of his old place of business (a honky-tonk) and the change had been hard on his red-nosed customers!

Another statement worthy of note is: "I've always tried to do the right thing. . . ." What a statement for a merchant of madness, a seller of sorrow, a companion of crime, a dispenser of death, to make!

Both the film company representative and the saloon-keeper should realize that God's mercy is not the effeminate sentimentalism of a doddering old woman. He is not unjust in mercy, but He must be both *"just*, and . . . *justifier,"* as we read in Romans 3:26. God's mercy cannot receive a single sinner into Heaven if that mercy overlooks the sinner's sin. *God cannot be unjust!*

The fourth person interviewed by Jemail was a Brooklyn typist. This girl replied: "I think so. I'm sure I'll have to make a local stop on the way, at a place called Purgatory, to be cleansed of my sins. In fact, I don't think there's a Hell. A God who is all good could not conceive of such a horrible place as a Hell where one would burn for eternity. God is mercy."

Here is amazement upon amazement, something to startle even old Beelzebub himself! This girl believes in a "Purgatory" *which God* DOESN'T *speak concerning,* but she refuses to believe in a Hell *of which He* DOES *speak!* The bold, blasphemous nerve of some people!

She lightly says, "A God who is all good . . ." and, "God is mercy." *But how does she know?* The same Bible which is our authority for His mercy also says, ". . . our God is a consuming fire" (Heb. 12:29). And, in describing the Son of God, it says, ". . . in righteousness he doth judge and make war. His eyes were as a flame of fire . . . . he was clothed with a vesture dipped in blood: and his name is called The Word of God. . . . out of his mouth goeth a sharp sword, that with it he should smite the nations: and he shall rule them with a rod of iron: and he treadeth the winepress of the fierceness and wrath of Almighty God" (Rev. 19:11-13, 15). This God of mercy is also a God of justice and judgment.

The fifth one interviewed, a Brooklyn salesman, said: "It isn't just as easy as saying yes or no. There's some doubt about it.

There's an old expression, 'Heaven for climate and Hell for company.' I've always preferred company to climate, and if that's the way it is, I'll be with many of my friends for a long time."

This is the answer of sarcastic infidelity and folly. Note two grievous errors in the salesman's banter: First, he said, "It isn't just as easy as saying yes or no." *But it is!* This question is as simply answered as one like, "Are you married?" or, "Do you have any children?" As a matter of fact, the only way it *can* be answered is by yes or no!

The second grievous error was when he laughingly quoted the expression, "Heaven for climate and Hell for company." There is no company, no companionship of any favorable sort in Hell. Hell is a land of torment and despair; a place completely devoid of any love or any enjoyment, regardless of its nature. The torments of Hell leave no room or hope for companionship!

The sixth and last person interviewed that day was a radio station worker. This lady replied to Jemail's query: "Only God knows that, but I have hopes. I've never killed anyone, I never stole anything and I have never desired another woman's husband. Of course that is all negative and I know I should do something positive to enter the sacred kingdom. I'm still very young and I hope I'll have a lot of time to think and act."

This resident of Manhattan made her first mistake in saying that "only God knows" who will go to Heaven. The Lord Jesus Christ made it perfectly clear to His disciples in Luke 10:20 that folks *could* and *should* know if they are Heaven-bound, and that the knowledge should bring great joy. Said He, "Notwithstanding in this rejoice not, that the spirits are subject unto you; but rather rejoice, because your names are written in heaven."

The beloved Apostle John added his inspired "Amen!" to this certainty when he wrote in I John 5:13, "These things have I written unto you that believe on the name of the Son of God; that ye may know that ye have eternal life, and that ye may believe on the name of the Son of God."

This sixth spokesman stated, "I have hopes," but all her hopes were based upon "works." She gloried in the fact that she had never killed, never stolen, and had never coveted another woman's husband. Future plans were only for piling up multiplied human "works of righteousness" to present to God as a basis for Heaven and eternal life.

Did you notice that of the six interviewed by the roving reporter, not a one even remotely referred to Jesus Christ? Yet our text in John 14 plainly declares that He alone is the way to Heaven. And as we read in Colossians 1:27, ". . . Christ in you, the hope of glory." Men without Christ are described by God as "having no hope" (Eph. 2:12). They have nothing to base their confidence upon, whether "mercy," "justice," "works," "righteousness," "God is good," "God is love," or anything else! *Any way which leaves out Christ ends in destruction — it is the way of death, doom and damnation!*

Last year a reliable, independent research firm took a nationwide survey of the religious habits and beliefs of Americans. Their figures showed that 99% believed in God. I think it would be fair to say that the very great majority of this number, if not all, feel that they will someday enter some kind of a Heaven prepared by this God. Yet, what saith the Scripture?

In His famous Sermon on the Mount, the Son of God emphatically stated, "Enter ye in at the strait gate: for wide is the gate, and broad is the way, that leadeth to destruction, and many there be which go in thereat: Because strait is the gate, and narrow is the way, which leadeth unto life, and few there be that find it." In language just as plain as day, our Saviour said that the vast majority of people reaching the age of accountability would be lost and end in Hell, that only a few would be saved and go to Heaven!

A few weeks ago an elderly lady became indignant over my remark that most of the people in the world were "bad." She bluntly stated that she much preferred to think the majority of her fellow men were good people. If I followed preference, I would think the same; but to follow the Scriptural teaching that it is impossible to call an unsaved man good and that most of mankind remains unsaved, it is necessary to admit man's depravity.

But in answering, Scripturally, the *New York Daily News'* all-important question, "Do You Think You Will Go to Heaven When You Die?" let us observe first of all,

I. ONLY GOD CAN SAY WHO WILL ENTER HEAVEN

He has the right of *ownership* — *it is His Heaven!* No one else has the right to tell another what he can do with his own property. I cannot tell you who can enter your home, who can live in your house; nor can you tell me who should be permitted to enter my home or live with me there. In exactly the same manner no mortal has the right to tell God what He can or cannot do with His heavenly home, who can live there for eternity or who must be barred.

God built Heaven Himself. He has a clear title to the four-square city; there is no mortgage, no claim against it by anyone. He prepared it especially for His own, for those who would lovingly accept Jesus Christ as their personal Saviour and Lord. You may be sure He will permit no intruder taking over that which has been prepared for His love! Would you? Neither will He!

You see, dear friend, God can make entrance into Heaven upon any ground He so desires. The sovereignty of God insists that He take counsel from no one, that none "instruct Him" or "show to him the way of understanding" (Isa. 49:13, 14). It would be well to read and reread Romans 9:14-24, noting especially the twentieth verse: "Nay but, O man, who art thou that repliest against God? Shall the thing formed say to him that formed it, Why hast thou made me thus?"

Whether you like His way or not, *it is final!* Your dislike or disagreement doesn't change it or alter it. In all love and with deep tenderness, I suggest you go God's way. *Trust Christ!*

Another Bible truth important to remember as we seek to answer Jimmy Jemail's question is,

II. GOD PROVIDES ONLY ONE WAY TO ENTER HEAVEN

There never has been but one way for deliverance and that is *God's way!* The Word of God abounds with illustrations of of this truth. For example, there was no deliverance in Noah's day except by God's way — *inside the Ark!* There was no deliverance in Moses' day but by God's way — *blood on the door-post!* There was no deliverance in Rahab's day but through God's way — *a scarlet cord hanging from the window.* Neither was there deliverance in Lot's day but by God's way — *fleeing the cursed city ripe for judgment of wrath.*

What was true in days of old is still true today. Men must go to Heaven *God's way* if they are to go at all. Futile and foolish are men's attempts to reach the streets of gold by fasting, by reciting prayers or counting beads, by human sacrifices, by payments of money to priests or churches, by baptisms or church memberships, by lodge rites or community charities, or by any effort of "works" on their part. *It cannot be done!*

A. *God's Way Only through His Son*

God's way is only through Christ. Our text records the words of God the Son: "I am the way, the truth, and the life: no man cometh unto the Father, but by me." You cannot reject Him and go to Heaven! Acts 4:12 insists, "Neither is there salvation in any other: for there is none other name under heaven given among men, whereby we must be saved."

B. *God's Way Only by Grace through Faith*

Furthermore, God's way through Christ is only by grace through faith. As we read in Ephesians 2:8, 9, "For by grace are ye saved through faith; and that not of yourselves: it is the gift of God: Not of works, lest any man should boast." Hebrews 11:6 adds, "But without faith it is impossible to please him: for he that cometh to God must believe that he is, and that he is a rewarder of them that diligently seek him."

People are not saved by "living right" or by "doing good." They are saved only as they put their entire hope in the Lamb of God, even Christ Jesus. We read God's appraisal of man's salvation in Titus 3:5-7, "Not by works of righteousness which we have done, but according to his mercy he saved us, by the washing of regeneration, and renewing of the Holy Ghost; Which he shed on us abundantly through Jesus Christ our Saviour; That being justified by his grace, we should be made heirs according to the hope of eternal life."

That salvation, and therefore Heaven, is gained by simple faith is seen in scores of Scriptures. Samples which could be cited in John alone are:

> But as many as received him, to them gave he power to become the sons of God, even to them that believe on his name. . . . And as Moses lifted up the serpent in the wilderness, even so must the Son of man be lifted up: That whosoever believeth

in him should not perish, but have eternal life. For God so loved the world, that he gave his only begotten Son, that whosoever believeth in him should not perish, but have everlasting life. . . . He that believeth on him is not condemned: but he that believeth not is condemned already, because he hath not believed in the name of the only begotten Son of God. . . . He that believeth on the Son hath everlasting life: and he that believeth not the Son shall not see life; but the wrath of God abideth on him. . . . Verily, verily, I say unto you, He that believeth on me hath everlasting life. . . . But these are written, that ye might believe that Jesus is the Christ, the Son of God; and that believing ye might have life through his name (John 1:12; 3: 14-16, 18, 36; 6:47; 20:31).

The word "believe" is set forth as the only condition of salvation more than one hundred times in the New Testament. The same New Testament uses the word "faith" some thirty-five times to describe this way of forgiveness and pardon. Altogether the two words are found one hundred and fifty times in the New Testament alone as the only condition of salvation.

D. L. Moody tells of a woman who came to him saying, "You are always saying, 'Take,' 'Take.' Is that all there is to salvation? Is that what God says or what you say?" The great evangelist took his Bible, turning to the closing pages as he said, "Madam, God has sealed His Word with the invitation to 'take.' Almost the last verse in the Bible says, 'And the Spirit and the bride say, Come. And let him that heareth say, Come. And let him that is athirst come. And whosoever will, let him *take* the water of life freely."

Yes, our blessed Lord simply says, "Let him take." When He says "take," dare any mortal deny that salvation is a gift assured and received the moment the sinner will only accept it? The way to Heaven is the road of grace made personal and sure by faith.

C. *God's Way Only through the New Birth*

The way to Heaven is further defined in the third chapter of John as being only through the new birth. Jesus said in John 3:3, "Verily, verily, I say unto thee, Except a man be born again, he cannot see the kingdom of God." He said moreover, "Except a man be born of water and of the Spirit, he cannot enter into the kingdom of God. That which is born of the flesh is flesh; and that which is born of the Spirit is spirit. Marvel not that I said unto thee, Ye must be born again" (John 3:5-7).

If you could be born of your mother's womb the second time, or the hundredth time, or the thousandth time, it would be of no avail — you would still be born of the flesh. Jesus said that in order to gain Heaven you must be born of the Spirit. He answered the question raised by Nicodemus as to "how" this might be possible by describing His death on the Cross and assuring those who would "believe" on Him that the requirement for the new birth would be thus met. Said He, "And as Moses lifted up the serpent in the wilderness, even so must the Son of man be lifted up: That whosoever believeth in him should not perish, but have eternal life" (John 3:14, 15).

One more Bible observation we must make in answering the *News'* question, "Do You Think You Will Go to Heaven When You Die?" is,

III. THOSE WHO REFUSE GOD'S ONLY WAY WILL PERISH

The Word of God contains scores of examples illustrating this terrible truth. One of the plainest, perhaps, is that of the ten virgins, given by Christ in chapter 25 of Matthew. These virgins all pretended to be ready to meet the coming bridegroom but it turned out that only half were really prepared. Verses 10 through 12 state with finality the fate of these who had not properly met the conditions of the bridegroom's coming. We read: "And while they went to buy, the bridegroom came; and they that were ready went in with him to the marriage: and the door was shut. Afterward came also the other virgins, saying, Lord, Lord, open to us. But he answered and said, Verily I say unto you, I know you not." Thus were the foolish, unprepared virgins shut out from the fellowship and presence of the Lord.

Another noteworthy example is found in Matthew 7:21-23 where unsaved preachers and miracle-workers are shut out from Heaven. We read: "Not every one that saith unto me, Lord, Lord, shall enter into the kingdom of heaven; but he that doeth the will of my Father which is in heaven [that is, they must come God's way according to God's terms if they want to enter God's Heaven]. Many will say to me in that day, Lord, Lord, have we not prophesied in thy name? and in thy name have cast out devils? and in thy name done many wonderful works? And then will I profess unto them, I never knew you: depart from me, ye that work iniquity." Do you not agree that if preachers and miracle-workers cannot get into Heaven unless they come God's way, then no one can?

Twice in Luke 13 the Lord Jesus declared, "I tell you, Nay: but, except ye repent, ye shall all likewise perish." It is turn, or burn! Psalm 1:5, 6, in describing the two roads mankind travels, says, "Therefore the ungodly shall not stand in the judgment, nor sinners in the congregation of the righteous. For the Lord knoweth the way of the righteous: but the way of the ungodly shall perish." The sinner's road always leads to Hell, never Heaven.

In verse 17 of Psalm 9 we read, "The wicked shall be turned into hell, and all the nations that forget God." The end of the rebel trail is damnation in Hell; never does it curve around and wind up in Heaven.

Startlingly true are the words of the Lord spoken on the Mount in the Olivet discourse and recorded in Matthew 25: 41, 46: "Then shall he say also unto them on the left hand, Depart from me, ye cursed, into everlasting fire, prepared for the devil and his angels. . . . And these shall go away into everlasting punishment: but the righteous into life eternal."

Likewise are the words of terror summing up the Great Judgment Morning, found in the closing pages of the Bible, Revelation 20:14, 15, where we read, "And death and hell were cast into the lake of fire. This is the second death. And whosoever was not found written in the book of life was cast into the lake of fire."

The plain truth is that those who refuse to come God's way for salvation must spend eternity in the lake of fire. Well might you join in crying with Mary Kidder,

> Lord, I care not for riches, neither silver nor gold;
> I would make sure of Heaven, I would enter the fold.
> In the book of Thy kingdom, with its pages so fair,
> Tell me, Jesus, my Saviour, is my name written there?

Yet that very question is so simple to answer for yourself! The Book of Life simply contains the names of those who have eternal life. Those who do not have that everlasting life do not have their names recorded, of course. I John 5:12 tells us, "He that hath the Son hath life; and he that hath not the Son of God hath not life." It's as simple as that! If you have Christ, you have life and your name *is* written there. If you do not have Christ, you do not have life and your name is *not* recorded there. Which is true in your case? Is *your* name written there?

Typical reasoning on the part of those whose names are not thus recorded is that of the sixth person interviewed by Jimmy Jemail in answering the question of our subject. That lady, you remember, said, "I'm still very young and I hope I'll have a lot of time to think and act."

Most folks feel they have plenty of time to decide for Christ and Heaven. But what say the Scriptures? Proverbs 27:1 declares, "Boast not thyself of to morrow; for thou knowest not what a day may bring forth." Again God says in the same book, "He, that being often reproved hardeneth his neck, shall suddenly be destroyed, and that without remedy" (Prov. 29:1). And Ecclesiastes 12:1 warns, "Remember now thy Creator in the days of thy youth, while the evil days come not, nor the years draw nigh, when thou shalt say, I have no pleasure in them."

The language of the Bible is always *"now," "today,"* and kindred expressions when describing God's time for salvation. The devil will agree to any other time but God always insists upon this moment. What about you today? Will you listen to God and trust Christ or will you manifest the folly of a person who listens to Satan?

One of the most striking gospel tracts I ever read contained the essence of a story told by a young paratrooper to Dr. Carl Henry in Chicago. It seems that this lad was one of ten taken high into the air in a giant training plane for their first jump. At the given signal the ten lined up at the door of the plane; he was the third in line.

The first man stepped to the door, paused, then bravely walked out into space. His chute opened and he later landed safely. The second man stepped to the door, paused, then stepped back, trembling, from the line. Then this third boy, who told Dr. Henry the story, bravely stepped to the door, paused, looked, and jumped. He, too, had a successful jump and a safe landing.

However, immediately after he cleared the plane, before another could leap, there was a terrific explosion and *every man aboard that plane perished,* including the boy who had been second in line but failed to leap. *He had missed his last chance!*

Dear unsaved friend, God is giving you a chance to step into His so great salvation, which includes that home in Heaven. Will you take it? *Don't miss your chance!*

I'm going to Heaven; I *know* that! Urgently, earnestly I beseech you to go with me. Will you? There is absolutely nothing to keep you from Heaven but your own rebellious will. You *can* be saved if you *will* be saved! "For whosoever shall call upon the name of the Lord shall be saved" (Rom. 10:13).

Delay for that young paratrooper meant death. Delay for you as a sinner may spell Hell! In the words of Britain's prince of preachers, "Hell is a reality realized *too late!*"

"In my Father's house are many mansions. . . . Thomas saith unto him, Lord . . . how can we know the way? Jesus saith unto him, *I am the way*" (John 14:2, 5, 6).

DECISION FOR CHRIST

Are you willing to come God's way to God's House? Surely you realize that He alone has the right to say who will enter Heaven and He has limited its inhabitants from earth to those who receive His Son as their Saviour! If you are willing to risk the Lord Jesus Christ to take you to Heaven, right now ask Him to come into your heart and then sign the decision form below as evidence of your heart surrender. Then copy the decision form or write me a letter in your own words telling of your victory. I will rejoice and send you some counsel and encouragement.

Evangelist Robert L. Sumner
P. O. Box 157
Brownsburg, Indiana 46112

Dear Brother Sumner:

I have just finished reading your Bible sermon, "Do You Think You Will Go to Heaven When You Die?" I admit that I am not good enough to go to Heaven on the basis of my own merit or righteousness. But I acknowledge the fact that Jesus Christ died in my place on the Cross to make salvation possible for me. Right now I am willing to put my soul into His holy hands and trust Him for a home in Heaven. I do believe He died for me and with His help I will live for Him.

Signed _____

Address _____

_____

HEAVEN. HOME, SWEET HOME, OF GOD'S CHILDREN

> We give thanks to God and the Father of our Lord Jesus Christ, praying always for you,
>
> Since we heard of your faith in Christ Jesus, and of the love which ye have to all the saints,
>
> For the hope which is laid up for you in heaven, whereof ye heard before in the word of the truth of the gospel;
>
> Which is come unto you, as it is in all the world; and bringeth forth fruit, as it doth also in you, since the day ye heard of it, and knew the grace of God in truth (Col. 1:3-6).

Note especially the fifth verse:

> For the hope which is laid up for you in heaven, whereof ye heard before in the word of the truth of the gospel.

While conducting an evangelistic crusade some time ago in western Pennsylvania, an emergency situation found me chauffering five members of the church to a cemetery for committal services. As we were about to go over the rise of a hill just outside the city, one of the ladies said, "Brother Sumner, notice the farm on the right side of the road when we get over the top of this hill." There I observed a very attractive farm with huge barns and a lovely old house. On the south of the original dwelling was a beautiful, new, spacious, ranch-style, brick home. This, they informed me, was the estate of a prosperous but profane gentleman who had compiled a considerable fortune specializing in cattle breeding.

One of the men who worked on the house during its construction later told me that $75,000 was his conservative estimate of its cost. He also related how the proud cattle breeder had dropped to his knees to show him how far his hand would sink down into the lovely, plush, thick, wall-to-wall carpeting in the living room. Yet the ladies told me how the man had moved with his family into that elaborately furnished house a few weeks previously, lived there two days, then dropped dead of a heart attack at the city hall. *He had built himself a $75,000 mansion and lived in it just two days!*

How that incident impressed upon my mind again with renewed force the absolute importance of having my main home in Heaven and laying up my principal treasures in the land that is fairer than day! Thank God, anyone can have a home worth far more than a mere $75,000 and have it not just for two days, two years or even two hundred years, but while eternal ages roll on unending — *a home in Heaven!*

Did you ever stop to think how little the Word of God tells us about Heaven? It has much more to say about Hell and even what it does reveal about Heaven is mostly what won't be there, rather than what will. In the "no more's" of Revelation 21 we are told there will be no more crying, no more pain, no more death, no more sickness, no more sorrow, no more temple, no more sun, no more moon, no more night and no gates shut by day. Frankly, we are not told very much about Heaven in the Bible.

However, what we are told is tremendous! It is as Job said about God, "Which doeth great things past finding out; yea, and wonders without number" (Job 9:10). There are great things about Heaven past finding out and wonders without number; yet God has seen fit to reveal only a limited few of them for us. Apparently He does not want us to know *too much* about that paradise He has prepared.

In II Corinthians 12:2-4 Paul refers to a man who once went to Heaven and returned. Most Bible students feel he was talking about an experience he himself had when he was stoned and left for dead outside the city of Lystra. But regardless of who the man was, Paul described it: "I knew a man in Christ above fourteen years ago, (whether in the body, I cannot tell; or whether out of the body, I cannot tell: God knoweth;) such an one caught up to the third heaven. And I knew such a man, (whether in the body, or out of the body, I cannot tell: God knoweth;) How that he was caught up into paradise, and heard unspeakable words, which it is not lawful for a man to utter."

Paul said, in essence, "I was caught up into Heaven, into

Paradise, and I saw unspeakable things. I would love to tell
you all about it but God won't let me. The things I saw and
the things I heard in Heaven He will not permit me to write
in this letter and describe for you." But while God has pur-
posely withheld much information about Heaven from us, the
things He *has* revealed — as we are reminded in Deuteronomy
29:29 — belong "unto us and to our children for ever. . . ."

In this message I want us to look into the precious Word
of God and consider some of those things He has revealed
about "the hope which is laid up for you in heaven." Let me
paint a few scenes, if I can, upon the canvas of your mind
to better acquaint you with this land the Bible calls Paradise,
Heaven, the Father's House and the New Jerusalem.

First of all,

I. HEAVEN — A HOME REAL AND PERMANENT

The Lord Jesus Christ told His disciples, "Let not your heart
be troubled: ye believe in God, believe also in me. [In other
words, 'You had faith in the Jehovah of the Old Testament;
believe in Me just as you believed in Him.'] In my Father's
house are many mansions: if it were not so, I would have told
you. I go to prepare a place for you. And if I go and prepare
a place for you, I will come again, and receive you unto myself; that where I am, there ye may be also" (John 14:1-3).

Heaven is *a place!* He said, "I go to prepare *a place* for you"
— a real, literal, eternal place — "if it were not so, I would have
told you." Someone has observed that Heaven is a prepared
place for prepared people, *and it is!* It is being prepared by
the Saviour for a people who themselves have been prepared
by a regeneration which made them new creations in Christ
Jesus. It is a place being readied by the Son of God for those
who have put their faith and trust in Him and had their sins
washed away by the blood of the Lamb slain 1900 years ago.
Yes, Heaven is a prepared place.

But Heaven is more than just a place, it is *a perfect place.*
Anyone who realizes what God can do, who understands anything at all about His omnipotent power, knows Heaven would
have to be a perfect place if He prepared it. God has never
blundered yet; the Lord Jesus has never once made a mess
of anything He set out to do. And you may be sure He will

not make a failure concerning Heaven. It will be a perfect place.

Heaven will be perfect in the sense that nothing will ever mar it. There will never be anything to defile it or spoil it. In Revelation 21, after describing some of the glories of Heaven, God says: "And there shall in no wise enter into it anything that defileth, neither whatsoever worketh abomination, or maketh a lie: but they which are written in the Lamb's book of life" (v. 27). Heaven is "off limits" to sin and sinners of every kind and description. Satan will never enter Heaven. The demons will never enter Heaven. The fallen angels who kept not their first estate will never enter Heaven. Unredeemed, unregenerate, Christ-rejecting mankind will never enter Heaven. God has promised that nothing to defile, nothing to spoil, nothing to work abomination will ever enter that celestial city.

When God created our domain He said of everything He had made — the earth, man, animals, all of it — "it is good!" And this earth, with all its inhabitants, *was* perfect in its original creation. But then Satan the spoiler, the deceiver, the worker of abomination entered to sow his handiwork of ruin. It was through this rising and entrance of sin by the master planning of Satan that God's perfect earthly creation was spoiled. But Satan the serpent will never rear his ugly head in His holy Heaven! God's arch-enemy will never have an opportunity to lead astray through subtlety the inhabitants of Glory! Nothing will ever enter to spoil it. Nothing will ever enter to sin. Heaven will be absolutely perfect in that sense.

Not only so, but Heaven will be perfect in the sense that there will be nothing lacking, nothing left out. We, like the Pennsylvania cattle breeder mentioned at the beginning of this message — though possibly not to such an elaborate, expensive extent — build our dream houses here on this earth. We plan, we scheme, we labor for months or years to draw up blueprints for a house we think will be ideal. But as soon as it's finished and we have moved in we sadly discover one of the doors opens the wrong way, or a closet is on the wrong side of the room, or a door is in the wrong place, or there ought to be a door where there is not one. We are not in our earthly dream houses long before the faults and flaws become obvious.

But there are no flaws, no faults, no mistakes in the home up yonder.

Heaven is perfect, too, in the sense of its glories, its beauties, its wonders. When you think a little bit about walls of crystal clear jasper, when you meditate just a moment about gates of solid pearl, when you ponder about streets of pure gold just like transparent glass, when you let the realization of these tremendous truths grip your heart and soul with the wonder of their loveliness, you will be constrained to shout with the amazement of the Southern singers, "How beautiful Heaven must be!"

When you consider one small pearl the size of a bullet — worth several thousand dollars — and look at its perfection, then realize that each of the twelve gates of Glory is made out of one solid pearl going the tremendous distance of "an hundred and forty and four cubits" straight up and absolutely free from a single flaw, when you think of their combined brilliance along with the Son of God reflecting upon them in a greater glory than manifested by the sun in yonder sky, then contemplate the beauties of the river of life, the mansions that go to make up the city of God and the other indescribable glories of that wonderland, you begin to realize just a little bit how perfect Heaven must be in the sense of glory, splendor, wonder and beauty.

But Heaven is not only a place, not only a perfect place, it is *a permanent, perfect place.* We are reminded in Hebrews 13:14, "For here have we no continuing city, but we seek one to come." There have been no continuing cities on this earth nor will there ever be. Think of Athens, Carthage, Babylon, Nineveh, Corinth and other mighty, splendorous, fascinating cities of days gone by. One by one they have crumbled into decay; all have either fallen completely or they possess only a shadow of their former glory. Then think of Moscow, London, New York, Washington, Berlin, Paris, Tokyo, Chicago and other present world centers, realizing that the day is approaching when they, too, shall be no longer. The time is coming when they will have crumbled into nothingness and even their memory forgotten.

Yet God's city will stand forever! It will abide permanently and there will be no crumbling, no decay, no wasting away, no conquering, no ruining of that city. This is a permanent abiding place, an eternal, continuing city. No wonder Hattie Buell wrote,

> A tent or a cottage, why should I care?
> They're building a palace for me over there;
> Tho' exiled from home, yet, still I may sing;
> All glory to God, I'm a child of the King.

Now let me give you another Scriptural scene:

II. HEAVEN — A HAVEN OF REST

We are told in Hebrews 4:9, "There remaineth therefore a rest to the people of God."

For one thing, there will be *rest from sin*. Revelation 21:27 declares: "And there shall in no wise enter into it any thing that defileth, neither whatsoever worketh abomination, or maketh a lie: but they which are written in the Lamb's book of life."

I John 3:2 delves deeper into the truth when it says: "Beloved, now are we the sons of God, and it doth not yet appear what we shall be: but we know that, when he shall appear, we shall be like him; for we shall see him as he is." As far as sin and our sinful natures are concerned, they will be gone forever! This corruption will put on incorruption, this mortality will put on immortality, and our sinful natures of wrath and woe will be destroyed completely. Richard Baxter well expressed it:

> My knowledge of that life is small,
> The eye of faith is dim,
> But 'tis enough that Christ knows all,
> And I shall be like Him.

The Lord Jesus Christ never committed a single sin and we shall be like Him. He never spake ill-advisedly with His lips nor was ever found with guile in His mouth. He never failed in a single thing the Father instructed Him to do. He never had an impure thought or committed an unholy act. He never sinned in any way, at any place, at any time, under any circumstance. *And we will be like Him!* When we enter into the city of God all sin and failure will be forever behind us. Our nature of sin will have been destroyed and only the divine nature which was imparted to us through the new birth will remain.

How many, many times we are compelled to seek out our secret closets and, on our knees with faces bathed in tears, confess our sins. Time and time again — altogether too often for the same sins and repeated iniquities — we have been forced to acknowledge our failures. We have had to admit, times without number, that He has given us some fort to hold and we failed to hold it. He has given us battles to fight, strongholds to conquer, victories to win — and we let Him down completely. But in Heaven there will be no failures, no need to confess sin. There will never be another time during all the endless eternity when tears will stain our cheeks because of our wrongdoing. Heaven is a place of rest from sin.

Not only so, Heaven is also a place of *rest from labor*. It tells us in Revelation 14:13, "And I heard a voice from heaven saying unto me, Write, Blessed are the dead which die in the Lord from henceforth: Yea, saith the Spirit, that they may rest from their labours; and their works do follow them."

Negroes in the South expressed this thought in song as they worked in the fields, singing,

> Goin' t' lay down my sword and shield,
> Down by the river-side,
> Down by the river-side,
> Goin' t' lay down my sword and shield,
> Down by the river-side,
> Goin' to study war no more.

One of these days you and I who know Christ as our personal Saviour will lay our sword and shield down by the riverside and step over into Glory, either through the valley of the shadow of death or in the rapture of the children of God at Christ's coming. Then we will study war no more — no more battles, no more fighting unrighteousness, no more launching all-out attacks against the forces of Satan — and all our battle cries will be changed into songs of peace and victory.

We will rest also from *sorrow*. In that lovely land there will be sweet rest from crying, disappointments, heartaches and the kindred woes which dog our path on earth. Revelation 21:4 tells us about Heaven: "And God shall wipe away all tears from their eyes; and there shall be no more death, neither sorrow, nor crying, neither shall there be any more pain: for the former things are passed away."

Our plans often go astray down here. How many disappointments we have, how much heartache, how many tears, how much grief caused by separation and sin! But we will have no more tears, no crying there. Someone has suggested that our glorified bodies will not have tear glands since we will have no need for them. The Lamb Himself will wipe away the last tear from our eyes and sadness will be no more.

Then, as Revelation 21:4 further indicates, we will also have *rest from pain and physical suffering.* How much sickness and disease, physical affliction, deformity and things of kindred nature we suffer in this life. But in Heaven they will be gone forever. Romans 8:18, 19 tells us about the redemption of our bodies: "For I reckon that the sufferings of this present time are not worthy to be compared with the glory which shall be revealed in us. For the earnest expectation of the creature waiteth for the manifestation of the sons of God."

Anyone familiar at all with suffering and physical affliction — one who has walked up and down the corridors of our hospitals and sanitariums, one who has seen the contagious disease wards and others places with the tremendous pain and oftentimes unbearable physical anguish that human beings, even children of God, are called upon to pass through — must marvel exceedingly at the extent of this glorious promise. We are told that the very worst physical suffering possible to endure in this life is not worthy of comparison with the glory which shall be hereafter, since that glory will be so exceedingly wonderful.

II Corinthians 4:17 tells us the same thing: "For our light affliction, which is but for a moment, worketh for us a far more exceeding and eternal weight of glory." Yes, this light affliction in the form of physical suffering and physical pain is just a *temporary thing!* Contrasted with eternity, it is "but for a moment." Compared with the glory of Heaven the affliction we now may have, no matter how great, is still a "light affliction." And that light affliction is working for the patient child of God who is submissive to His will, even in suffering, a far more exceeding and eternal weight of glory. In Heaven with a perfect body, with no more pain or physical affliction, we will rest in Him forever. Oh, thank God, if you can sing,

> I've anchored my soul in the Haven of Rest,
> I'll sail the wide seas no more;
> The tempest may sweep o'er the wild, stormy deep,
> In Jesus I'm safe evermore.

Yes, in the Son of God we have a safe haven of rest here, but a wonderful, glorious haven of rest hereafter.

Think with me again about another scene in that celestial city:

III. HEAVEN — A HARMONY OF MUSIC

Song is a manifestation of joy, an almost spontaneous manifestation of joy. Happy people *must* sing. Sometimes that song is outward with their lips, sometimes only inwardly in their hearts, but happy people love to sing and that song is an evidence, a proof of joy.

As a sample of what the Word of God tells us about the sweet music and joy of Heaven, the Apostle John says in Revelation 5:11, 12: "And I beheld, and I heard the voice of many angels round about the throne and the beasts and the elders: and the number of them was ten thousand times ten thousand, and thousands of thousands, Saying with a loud voice, Worthy is the Lamb that was slain to receive power, and riches, and wisdom, and strength, and honour, and glory, and blessing." John, getting his preview of Heaven while imprisoned on the isle of Patmos, saw and heard ten thousand times ten thousand (that is, one hundred million), plus thousands of thousands, praising the Lamb that was slain.

What a choir!

Not long ago I read of a choir in Europe which boasted five thousand trained voices blending in songs of praise to the Son of God. Yet how insignificant even a five-thousand-voice choir would sound in contrast to the melody of Heaven when the saints begin to sing praises in a manner fitting the might, majesty and mercy of Jesus Christ! Try to imagine, if you will, one hundred million, plus thousands of thousands of perfectly pitched melodious voices! No one will be off-key; everyone will be in perfect harmony. That ideal choir will feature the beautiful melody of stringed instruments blending with voices that have been redeemed, purified and made perfect by the power of Almighty God in the new creation.

Yes, Heaven will be a harmony of music! Everyone will be happy over there; all will be sweetly singing songs to honor their Saviour. Even voices that knew no tone or pitch on earth will be singing in beautiful harmony along with all the rest. How beautiful and wonderful Heaven must be!

But let me paint you another scene of that permanent paradise:

IV. HEAVEN — A HABITATION WITH GOD

When Harry Monroe, faithful leader of the noted Pacific Garden Mission in the city of Chicago, died, Dr. James M. Gray read the following poem by Annie Johnson Flint at his funeral:

> 'Tis not the golden streets,
> 'Tis not the pearly gates,
> 'Tis not the perfect rest
> For weary hearts that wait,
> 'Tis not that we shall find
> The joy earth has not given,
> For which our souls have longed,
>   That makes it Heaven.
>
> But 'tis because we know
> Our Saviour King is there
> With all our loved and lost
> In that blest land and fair;
> That when to each of us
> A place prepared is given,
> His face and theirs we'll see,
>   That makes it Heaven.

Revelation 21:3 tells us concerning the city of God: "And I heard a great voice out of heaven saying, Behold, the tabernacle of God is with men, and he will dwell with them, and they shall be his people, and God himself shall be with them, and be their God." Notice especially the words, "the tabernacle of *God* is *with men*," and again, "*he* will dwell *with them*," and yet again,"*God himself* shall be *with them*." The greatest thing about Heaven is right here: *The children of God will be with Jesus Christ forever!*

The greatest thing about Heaven will not be our rewards —

the crowns, the spotless white robes, or the trophies representing our faithful service to Jesus Christ. The greatest thing about
Heaven will not be in meeting the heroes of the faith like
Daniel, Paul, Abraham, Peter, Moses, Stephen, Elijah, or such
stalwarts of the centuries as Augustine, Luther, Wesley, Torrey,
Moody, Sunday and Spurgeon. Nor will the greatest thing
about Heaven even be the reunion with our loved ones as we
greet fathers, mothers, brothers, sisters, sons, daughters, husbands or wives who had gone on before. *The greatest thing
about Heaven will be our union and fellowship with the Son
of God, the Lord Jesus Christ, our Saviour and Redeemer!* As
Mrs. Frank Breck taught us to sing:

> Only faintly now I see Him,
> With the darkling veil between;
> But a blessed day is coming,
> When His glory shall be seen.
>
> Face to face shall I behold Him,
> Far beyond the starry sky;
> Face to face in all His glory,
> I shall see Him by and by!

No other joy of Heaven will exceed or even begin to compare
with that of our being with Jesus Christ and having communion
with Him.

One of America's greatest preachers and orators was a Negro
by the name of John Jasper. He preached years ago in Rich-
mond, Virginia, and Dr. T. T. Martin called him the greatest
orator — preacher or politician, black or white — who ever lived in
America. Thousands, both Negro and white, jammed his church
Sunday after Sunday to hear him preach. They came from every
state in the Union. They came from every country in Europe.
They came from the uttermost parts of the earth to hear him
passionately and eloquently tell the wonderful story of Christ's
redeeming love and grace.

One Sunday morning this saint who had been born a slave
and raised a slave was telling his hearers about the glories
of Heaven. As he preached he became so completely overcome
with emotion that he could not control himself and simply stood
in the pulpit weeping like a child. Finally he made a motion
with his hand to dismiss the congregation and with shoulders

stooped over made his way across the platform to the study door. Then, as he laid his hand on the knob, he stopped, gained control of his emotions by sheer determination and will, turned back to the rostrum, leaned over the pulpit and began talking to the people once again.

"Beloved," he said, "one of these days old John Jasper is going to die. I'm going to walk down the streets of Glory and an angel will come up to me and say, 'John Jasper, don't you want your robe that was made white by the blood of the Lamb, the robe King Jesus has provided for you?'

"Then I'll say, 'Yes, Marse Angel, I certainly do want that robe that was made white by the blood of the Lamb which Jesus provided for me, but first of all, I want to see Jesus; I want to see my Saviour.'

"I'll walk on down the golden streets a little bit farther and another angel will meet me and he will say, 'John Jasper, don't you want that golden crown that's bedecked with all the jewels representing the souls you won to Jesus?'

"And I'll say to him, 'Yes, Marse Angel, I sure do want that golden crown with all the jewels representing my soul-winning efforts for the Master; but first of all, I want to see Jesus and fall down prostrate before His nail-pierced feet, kiss those holes that were made because of my transgressions, and thank Him with a burning heart for saving such a poor, wicked, miserable, black sinner as I.'"

You and I may not agree with some of the details of John Jasper's theology about whom he will see first when he gets to Heaven, but every born-again child of God says a burning "Amen" from a passionate heart to his philosophy of wanting to see Jesus first! Oh, what a wonderful Saviour is He to save such double-dyed, iniquity-soaked, transgression-polluted, in-for-Hell sinners as you and I! How wonderful it will be when we look upon Him whom, having not seen, we love with all our heart.

> Oh, the dear ones in glory, how they beckon me to come,
>   And our parting at the river I recall;
> To the sweet vales of Eden they will sing my welcome home,
>   But I long to meet my Saviour first of all.

Yes, Heaven will be a habitation with God when we will dwell with Him, live with Him, and where fellowship and communion will never be broken a single time. Throughout all eternity we will be with our blessed Saviour and Redeemer.

Now let me paint another scene for you upon the canvas of your mind:

V. HEAVEN — A HOLY COMPLETION OF KNOWLEDGE

There are a lot of things we don't know now — admittedly many of them things we ought to know — but the day is coming when our knowledge will be perfect. I Corinthians 13:12 tells us: "For now we see through a glass, darkly; but then face to face: now I know in part; but then shall I know even as also I am known." We have only partial knowledge now but complete knowledge is God's promise for our future.

I think it is significant that this statement about knowledge is found in the chapter universally recognized as the great love chapter of the Bible. It is partly because of God's love that we do not know a good many things now and that a great many details relative to life and service He keeps hidden from us. On the other hand, it is partly because of His love that one day our knowledge will be completed and made full.

> When the mists have rolled in splendor
> From the beauty of the hills,
> And the sunlight falls in gladness
> On the river and the rills,
> We recall our Father's promise
> In the rainbow of the spray:
> We shall know each other better
> When the mists have rolled away.

This truth answers for us the question so many people ask, "Will we know each other in Heaven?" Yes, *we will!* If we know our loved ones now with only partial knowledge, we will surely know them when our knowledge has been made complete.

In this life we get acquainted with people through introductions and after other formalities have taken place, but over yonder we shall know without any introductions or formalities. The heroes of the Cross whom we have never known will be recognized immediately and they in turn will recognize us. An illustration of this truth is seen in the recognition by Peter of both Moses and Elijah on the Mount of Transfiguration although no formalities of introduction transpired.

Every individual in Heaven will have complete, perfect knowledge. What a wonderful time of fellowship and communion will be ours when the introverts and the extroverts will be afflicted no longer. Each will know as he is known and will in turn be known with perfect knowledge.

When our knowledge is made complete we will understand why darkness instead of sunshine was over so many a cherished plan. We will know — *and see it was best* — why some of the programs we wanted to put through for God never were realized because of the limiting, restraining hand which held us back. The Josephs will understand the rejection and mistreatment by their brethren. The Daniels will understand why in the program of God they were compelled to be cast into the lions' den. The Shadrachs, Meshachs, and Abednegos will understand why God thought it best to send them into the fiery furnace. The Jeremiahs and Peters and Pauls and Silases will understand their prison pit experiences and why it was necessary for them to be cast into dungeons for the testimony of their Lord.

We will understand why we were afflicted, why we were persecuted at times by both friend and foe alike, why it was necessary in the providence of God to endure trials and testings while here on earth. In the meantime, the best we can do is say with Job, "Though he slay me, yet will I trust in him. . . ." (13:15). Let come what may — whether victories or defeats, whether triumphs or heartaches, whether persecution or praise, whether blessing or discouragement — I'll trust in Him and walk by faith knowing that His will is wiser than my own, confident that He knows the end from the beginning and will not permit one thing to happen to me but what He will work together for my good. One day our knowledge will be complete and we will know the whys, the wherefores and the whens of all the things we have endured for the testimony of Jesus Christ on earth. Yes, Heaven will be a holy completion of knowledge.

Now let me give you another scene:

VI. HEAVEN — A HAPPY REUNION

What a joyous homecoming will be ours when we arrive on the other side to be greeted and reunited with friends and loved ones who have gone on before. We noted previously that the greatest thing about Heaven is not our loved ones but Christ — we will be with Him — and that is true. But it is also an added joy, an added blessing that we will be with our friends and loved ones. Perhaps it is a father who has gone on before or a mother we watched slip away to the other shore whom we are anxious to greet again. That husband or wife who had been with us through the toils, troubles, tribulations and heart-aches of so many years and preceded us in their coronation day, that baby who was laid away in innocent infancy, that son or daughter who fell in the prime of young manhood or young womanhood — we will be with them never to be separated again while the ages come and go. The Southern song writer expressed his anticipation over this awaited event with the words:

> We'll sing and shout and praise the Lord,
>> The Lamb will dry our tears;
> We'll have a grand homecoming week
>> The first ten thousand years.

And so we will! The blessed thought is that

> No parting word shall e'er be spoken
>> In that bright land so fair;
> But songs of joy and peace and gladness,
>> We'll sing for ever there.
> We'll never say good-by in Heaven,
>> We'll never say good-by;
> In that bright land of joy and song
>> We'll never say good-by.

Oh, beloved, think of it! We will never say good-by, never be separated at all, but be together forever. The important thought in this line of truth is, of course, that the circle be unbroken. Will all your family, your loved ones and your friends be reunited with you in Heaven? Will *you* be there? If unsaved, I beseech you right now to prepare for Heaven by faith in the Lord Jesus Christ so that the circle will not be

broken through your absence. If you already know Christ and
are Heaven-bound, yet have loved ones who are not converted,
oh, how earnestly you ought to pay the price in tears, in sup-
plication, in continued intercession at the throne of grace until
you see every loved one converted and the circle completed
on the other side. Heaven will be a happy homecoming, a glorious reunion.

But let me give you still another scene from the Scriptures
of that paradise:

VII. Heaven — a Heartbeat Away

Sometimes folks talk about Heaven as the "beautiful isle of
somewhere" and they sing of the place "far, far away," *but that
is not so!* The Bible presents the picture of Heaven as just one
heartbeat away and when the old heart beats for the final time
the individual who knows Christ as his personal Saviour will
step immediately into the presence of Almighty God in Glory.
Paul expressed this thought in Philippians 1:21, 23, 24, saying,
"For to me to live is Christ, and to die is gain. . . . For I am
in a strait betwixt two, having a desire to depart, and to be
with Christ; which is far better: Nevertheless to abide in the
flesh is more needful for you."

Paul said in essence, "I am deeply stirred between a twofold
decision. I would like to depart right now and be with the
Lord Jesus Christ. I would like to die and leave all the troubles,
trials, persecutions and perplexities of this life and step into
the presence of my Redeemer, never to leave Him. But on the
other hand it is much more needful for me to remain on this
earthly scene. There are so many churches that need to be
encouraged and built up in the faith and truth of God's Word.
The whole world is lost and dying and headed for an eternal
Hell. There are many who need to be converted and the Gospel
needs to be preached to the uttermost parts of the earth. I
would like to depart and be with Christ but it is much more
needful for me to stay right here." Paul could only say *"to
die is gain"* if the child of God goes to be with Christ the very
moment he dies. Dying is not soul-sleeping, it is awakening
with Jesus!

Do you remember that when Jesus was crucified there were
two thieves — one on either side — reviling, cursing and joining

with the disparagement of the crowd as they ridiculed and blasphemed Him? Then, suddenly, one of the thieves apparently got a better look at the Man on the middle cross and stopped his blaspheming and reviling to cry in faith, "Lord, remember me when thou comest into thy kingdom." And Luke 23:43 records the response, "Jesus said unto him, Verily I say unto thee, To day shalt thou be with me in paradise." That dying thief, who put his trust in the dying Saviour, was guaranteed *that very day* he would be in Heaven — without any delay or any waiting. The very moment he died he went to be with Jesus Christ in Paradise.

In the fifth chapter of II Corinthians Paul used the illustration of the body as a house or tabernacle where the soul and spirit — *the real you* — dwell. He said, "For we know that if our earthly house of this tabernacle were dissolved, we have a building of God, an house not made with hands, eternal in the heavens" (v. 1). The Word of God assures us that even though our bodies will be dissolved, in Heaven we will have bodies not made with hands, eternal bodies prepared for us by Almighty God Himself. Paul went on to say in the eighth verse of that same chapter, "We are confident, I say, and willing rather to be absent from the body, and to be present with the Lord."

What a wonderful truth: *"absent from the body . . . present with the Lord."* There is no purgatory, no soul sleeping, no waiting, no delay; the moment the soul and spirit of a Christian leave his body he goes immediately into the presence of his Saviour. It might be well to ask all who believe and teach soul sleeping: *When will the Christian be absent from the body if, as you say, the soul and spirit are laid away with the body until the resurrection morning and at that time body, soul and spirit are raised from the dead to stand in the presence of God?* The fact of the matter is that in such a false philosophy there could be no absenteeism from the body. But, thank God, for the Christian, the moment he dies he *is* absent from the body and he *is* present with the Lord. Heaven *is* just a heartbeat away for the saved!

I think of how, less than a month ago, I conducted funeral services for my own father. Dad came home that Tuesday night from a hard day's work, ate a big supper of chicken and biscuits — one of his favorite dishes — then spent the evening reading, eating a dish of ice cream before he retired. He had been telling his friends — and he was sincere and honest in his statement — that he had never felt better in his life. But less than an hour after my father went to bed, my mother heard him gasp for breath once or twice in his sleep — and his soul and spirit immediately departed from his body into the presence of the Saviour who had died for him and whom he long had been anxious to meet. Oh, how sudden, how unexpectedly that heart attack took him from this life into the presence of Almighty God!

What happened to my father has been multiplied a thousand times over in the days, weeks and months past as individual after individual has been hurled suddenly, without any warning whatsoever, out into eternity and the presence of God. *Oh, how serious this is!* How earnest and important it is that you be ready for the hour of death and departure! For those who are ready, Heaven is just a heartbeat away.

Let me give you one more picture of that land that is fairer than day:

VIII. HEAVEN — A HOPE SECURED IN CHRIST

Colossians 1:5 described it, "For the hope which is laid up for you in heaven, whereof ye heard before in the word of the truth of the gospel." This hope for Heaven is centered in *"the truth of the gospel."* It was only as the people of Colosse received the truth of the Gospel that they had a hope for Heaven.

What was the truth of the Gospel? What was their hope of Heaven? We are told in that same first chapter of Colossians, ". . . which is Christ in you, the hope of glory" (v. 27). The *only* hope any individual can have for Heaven is through Jesus Christ. There is no other hope; there is no other way. Morality, with all its good works, charitable acts and righteous deeds will not pave the way to Heaven. Religion, with all its ritualism and ordinances will not open the gates of Glory. There is only one way into Heaven and that is through receiving Jesus Christ into your heart by faith, thereupon being born again as His child.

Do you remember how, after telling the disciples about the Father's house of many mansions in the fourteenth chapter of

John, Jesus went on to say, ". . . whither I go ye know, and the way ye know"? Thomas replied immediately, and this is one time I'm thankful for Thomas' doubt since it caused Christ to give such a crystal clear answer about the way to Glory. Thomas said, "Lord, we know not whither thou goest; and how can we know the way?"

Jesus replied in verse 6, saying, "I am the way, the truth, and the life: no man cometh unto the Father, but by me." Jesus is the way to Heaven! He is the truth; He is the life! There is absolutely *no* other way to the Father but by Him. And all who do come by faith in Him will immediately receive eternal life and the guarantee of a heavenly home. Yes, Heaven *can be yours!*

Let me ask you the most important question it is possible for one mortal being to ask another: *Are you sure of Heaven?* Do you know beyond any question of a doubt that you have a clear title to a mansion in Glory? You *can* know it! The Word of God assures us, "These things have I written unto you that believe on the name of the Son of God; that ye may know that ye have eternal life . . ." (I John 5:13). It tells us also in John 3:16, "For God so loved the world, that he gave his only begotten Son, that whosoever believeth in him should not perish, but have everlasting life."

Right now, if you will believe in Him, you will *have* everlasting life. Revelation 3:20 pictures Christ knocking at the door of the heart, saying, "Behold, I stand at the door, and knock: if any man hear my voice, and open the door, I will come in to him, and will sup with him, and he with me."

Dear friend, the Lord Jesus Christ is knocking right now through this printed message at the door of your heart, saying, "Will you let Me in? Will you open the door? Will you permit Me entrance into your heart and life?" Right now, if you will honestly say in your heart, "Yes, Lord Jesus, I *will* open the door. You may come in. I will gladly receive You as my personal Saviour," you will be saved and saved forever! Remember, it is ". . . *Christ in you the hope of glory.*"

DECISION FOR CHRIST

Surely you want to make Heaven your eternal home! No one in his right mind would deliberately choose Hell and spurn

God's glorious Heaven. Yet, unless your sins are forgiven and Jesus Christ becomes your Saviour, you will miss Heaven and end up in Hell just as surely as if you had made Hell your deliberate choice. Jesus said, "Verily, verily, I say unto thee, Except a man be born again, he cannot see the kingdom of God . . . Marvel not that I said unto thee, Ye must be born again" (John 3:3, 7). You must be born again if you hope to see Heaven.

Why not trust Jesus and be born again right now? It is true that "as many as received him, to them gave he power to become the sons of God, even to them that believe on his name" (John 1:12), so if you will receive Him today you will immediately become a child of God. Will you receive Him? Will you believe on His Name? If so, sign the following decision form as an outward indication of your inward surrender, then write me a letter telling me you have let Christ into your heart.

Evangelist Robert L. Sumner
P. O. Box 157
Brownsburg, Indiana 46112

Dear Brother Sumner:

I have read your sermon, "Heaven: Home, Sweet Home, of God's Children!" Now I would like to become a child of God and make sure that Heaven will be my eternal home. Right now, as sincerely and honestly as I know how, I repent of my sins and ask the Lord Jesus Christ to come into my heart. I know I am a sinner and deserve Hell, but I will trust His grace to forgive me and save me. I trust Him to do it this moment.

Signed ....

Address ....

....

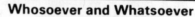

Some of Our Latest

Come Out or Stay In?

"Get it straight from the horse's mouth!" is wise counsel for anyone. Dr. Rice is caricatured variously along all lines of the theological spectrum today—all the way from being a rank modernist to a hell-raising, cantankerous isolationist. This comparatively recent paper-bound volume will set the records straight for anybody who is really interested in knowing the facts: not only as to what Dr. Rice's personal position is but, after reading this candid, impartial, unprejudiced presentation of the important issues involved, the reader will be thoroughly and properly instructed and informed on the Bible position that every honest Christian should want to take. 249 pages,

$3.95.

Preaching That Built a Great Church

By Dr. John R. Rice. 29 stenographically reported messages used of God to build a church of 1,700 members, with over 7,000 professions of faith, in the midst of the bitter depression times—1932-1940. With such preaching as this, Dr. Rice, under God, founded and built the Fundamentalist Baptist Tabernacle, now the Galilean Baptist Church in Dallas, Texas. Young preachers, this is the kind of specimen preaching that will put the old-time fire in the bones—you ought to read them! Every Christian ought to read them, and would profit immeasurably when he does. A colossal paperbound volume with perfect binding, 585 pages,

$3.95.

Sweet Family Ties in Heaven and Hell

By Dr. John R. Rice. In addition to the sermon that serves as title of this recent volume, there are other life-changing sermons preached in principal pulpits all over America. Some other titles are: "Come and See!" "All-Out Christians," "Helping Jesus Get a Man Saved," "Going Back," "Bold Preacher, Trembling Sinner," etc. There are 11 chapters in all. These are hot, extemporaneous messages, just as given from the pulpit, not cold addresses prepared in the private study. Each one has a message for saint and sinner alike. 222 pages, **$3.50.**

Our Newest Books

Building and Battling

. . .and Other Sermons, by Dr. Curtis Hutson, pastor of Forrest Hills Baptist Church of Decatur, Georgia. This one-time part-time mail-carrying preacher of a small congregation of less than 100, after exposure to THE SWORD OF THE LORD and a Sword Conference on Soul Winning and Revival, in 13 years has built that church to a membership of over 5,000, a Sunday school attendance of nearly 2,500, with a high of 5,138. This kind of Spirit-filled, dynamic preaching is what has helped to make the difference. 12 chapters, 186 clothbound pages.

$3.50.

The Lord's True Servants. . . and Other Sermons.

By Dr. Leon F. Maurer. Ouch!! This is so recently hot from the press it burns my fingers when I touch it for review! Excuse the hyperbola as we try to impress upon you the newness of this, our very most recent publication. But there is a sense in which it is no hyperbola to say that these sermons are hot from the warm heart of a fervent, fundamental, greatly-used man of God, now in the field of evangelism. There are 12 heart-moving messages in this clothbound volume of 151 pages.

$3.50.

100 Bill Harvey Poems

In his Introduction, Dr. R. G. Lee states:

"I have read some of the poems written by the Reverend Bill Harvey. Much pleasure and profit I received in reading them. These poems are exquisitely excellent—as all who read will know.

"These poems are not rills but rivers of truth. They are not mediocre hills but magnificent mountains of delineation of some Bible events.

"Especially fine is the poem that sets forth the David-Uriah tragedy that wrought havoc in the lives of David, Uriah, and Bathsheba. . . ."

Exactly 100 poems, artistic page layouts with pictures and drawings. Alphabetically indexed, attractively clothbound.

$2.95.